The New
MRS LEE'S
COOKBOOK

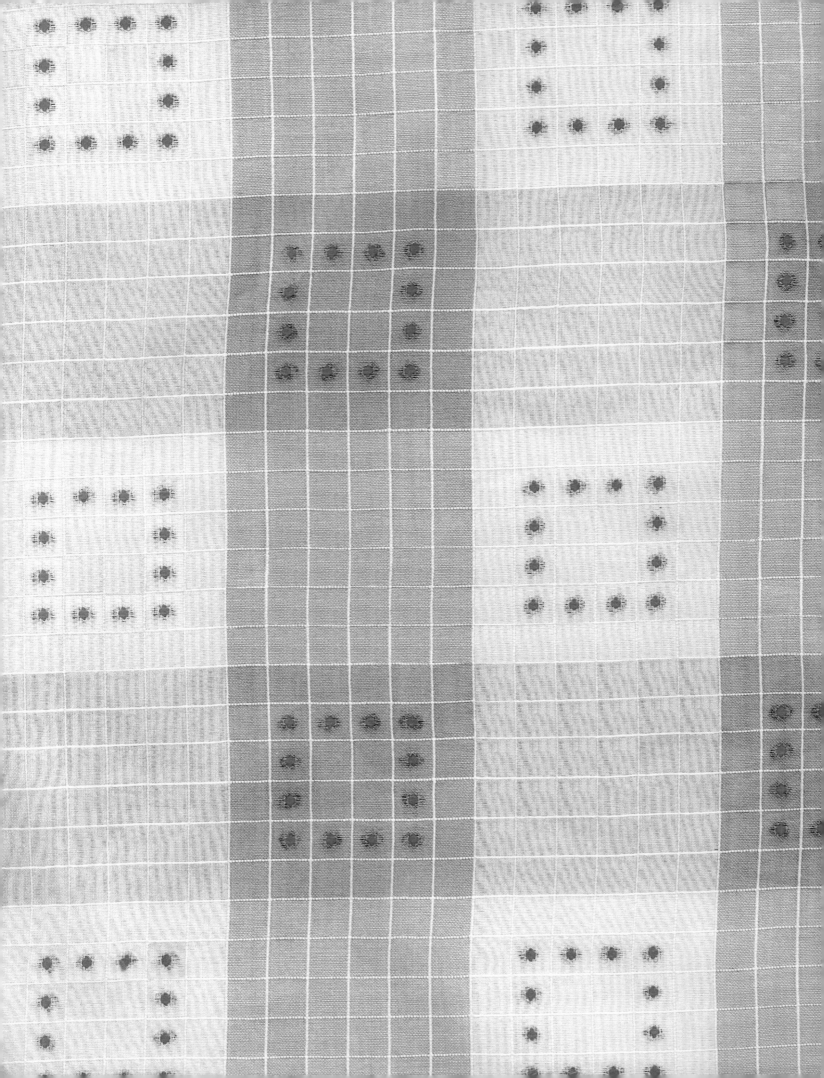

The New MRS LEE'S COOKBOOK

Nonya Cuisine

Written by **Mrs Lee Chin Koon**
Updated by her granddaughter **Shermay Lee**

TIMES EDITIONS

Food Preparation: Shermay Lee
Project Editor: Jamilah Mohd Hassan
Art Direction: David Yip
Designer: Lynn Chin Nyuk Ling
Photographer: Yu Hui Ying
Editor: Lydia Leong
Production Co-ordinator: Nor Sidah Haron

© 2003 Shermay Lee

Published by Times Editions
An imprint of Times Media Private Limited
A member of the Times Publishing Group

Times Centre, 1 New Industrial Road, Singapore 536196
Tel: (65) 6213 9288   Fax: (65) 6285 4871
E-mail: te@tpl.com.sg
Online Book Store: http://www.timesone.com.sg/te

Times Subang, Lot 46, Persiaran Teknologi Subang
Subang Hi-Tech Industrial Park, Batu Tiga, 40000 Shah Alam
Selangor Darul Ehsan, Malaysia
Tel: (603) 5628 6828 / 5635 2191
Fax: (603) 5636 4620 / 5635 2706
E-mail: cchong@tpg.com.my

National Library Board (Singapore) Cataloguing in Publication Data

Lee, Chin Koon, Mrs.
The new Mrs. Lee's cookbook : Nonya cuisine / written by Mrs. Lee Chin Koon ; updated by Shermay Lee. - Singapore : Times Editions, 2003.
p. cm.
ISBN : 981-232-704-5
ISBN : 981-232-761-4 (pbk.)

1. Cookery, Peranakan (Chinese) 2. Cookery, Singapore. I. Lee,
Shermay, 1975- II. Title.
TX724.5.S
641.595957 — dc21   SLS2003030725

Printed by Saik Wah Press Pte Ltd

Contents

Foreword

Time marches on. Even for cookbooks.

It has been 29 years since I wrote the preface to the first edition of *Mrs Lee's Cookbook*. At the time and now, Mrs Lee Chin Koon's proficiency in the kitchen is a well acknowledged fact, especially among those of us who were close enough to the 'cook' to benefit from the proximity. My mouth still waters at the mere thought of the many intricacies coming out of her kitchen.

Although time waits for no one, the flavours of Mrs Lee's recipes live on. For those intrepid adventurers into the kitchen, these flavours will be more than just a memory.

I am honoured to be asked again to write the foreword to this brand new edition, *The New Mrs Lee's Cookbook.* Even so, it is an honour I accept with much trepidation. As one who cannot boil an egg properly for breakfast or cook a pot of rice, what can I possibly say that would add to your pleasure?

This new edition promises a sumptuous spread of colour images and an informed text by Shermay Lee to accompany Mrs Lee's time-honoured recipes. After all, the pleasures from this particular book must surely be in the cooking! Readers will quickly recognise that Shermay is as equally proficient a writer as her grandmother was a cook. Shermay's introduction whets the appetite like a delicate serving of hors d'oeuvre.

It remains for me to have the pleasure and honour to present to you, Shermay Lee, granddaughter of the cook, herself trained at Le Cordon Bleu. To you who shall have the good fortune to hold this book in hand, I wish you many pleasurable hours.

Dr Wee Kim Wee
October 2003
Former President of the Republic of Singapore
(1985–1993)

This photograph captures a typical afternoon where my grandmother, aged 73 and I, aged 5, cooked in the kitchen of the house I grew up in. The *batu lesung* (mortar and pestle) that my grandmother is using is the same one that is still used every day in my home. Our black-and-white *amah* (maid), Ah Tong, is standing in the background.

Introduction

My grandmother, Mrs Lee Chin Koon, first published *Mrs Lee's Cookbook* in 1974. My mother, Pamelia Lee, assisted her by editing the cookbook. Almost three decades later, I am relaunching the famous cookbook.

The idea of relaunching the cookbook had been on my mind for a while and when I embarked on the project, I was fully aware of the responsibility that updating it entailed. My grandmother was considered an authority on Nonya cuisine and her cookbook has since become synonymous with Nonya cuisine. A whole generation has grown up with the familiar orange-coloured cookbook, and I felt it was important that the new edition remain authentic yet more accessible to a new generation of aspiring cooks.

In this new edition, the recipes are written in a step-by-step format and come complete with photographs to illustrate each dish. Few adjustments have been made to the recipes, except where I felt it necessary, to cater to modern taste buds and preferences. I have also included cooking tips, some from my aunts who have shared their secrets with me, and others based on my classic culinary training. In addition, there are anecdotes about the dishes and suggestions on preparing healthier versions of these Peranakan classics.

I am a sixth-generation Peranakan and I grew up enjoying these dishes at home. More importantly, during the first five years of my life, I spent much time with my grandmother, whom I affectionately called 'Mak', or 'Mama Lee' as she was known to many. She instilled in me a passion for cooking from a very young age. As a child, I would often spend the afternoon by her side while she cooked dinner or special dishes as requested by the family. My father's favourite requests were Mee Siam, Ayam Buah Keluak and Pong Tauhu Soup.

This cookbook pays homage to my grandmother and would be, I believe and hope, a fulfillment of her wish to make authentic Peranakan dishes accessible to the generations after her. In the introduction to *Mrs Lee's Cookbook*, she commented, "it has been one of my ambitions to write a book about Straits Chinese food so that the younger generation, including my grandchildren and later their grandchildren, will have access to these recipes which were usually kept within families as guarded secrets." It will be most rewarding to see well-thumbed, dogged-eared copies of this new edition in the kitchen of young households. It will signify that my grandmother's legacy is alive and well.

Shermay Lee
October 2003

Acknowledgments

A project such as this would not have been possible without the help and encouragement of many friends, family and professionals. The completion of this cookbook is a dream and passion.

INGREDIENTS

My grandmother

My parents

Sherlyn, Kern and Shaun

The team at Times Media

Easycam Services

Wee Kim Wee

Kay Kuok

Irene Ooi

Tina Lee

Rachel Ong

Margaret Chew

Ong Ker Shing

Richard Lee

PREPARATION

1 This book is possible only because my grandmother was such a dynamic woman and talented cook. She was a wonderful grandmother and my memories of her will always be fond.

2 My parents, who have supported and encouraged me. Special thanks to my mother who edited the original edition and handed down this legacy to me.

3 My siblings, Sherlyn, Kern and Shaun. Thank you for your love and support.

4 The team at Times Media: Elsa Tan, David Yip, Lydia Leong, Jamilah Mohd Hassan, Tan Joo Sin, Lynn Chin, Audrey Chow and Kay Woon Chuen.

5 My photography team: Yu Hui Ying and Lek Hui Hui

6 Dr Wee for your kind words.

7 Dearest Aunty Kay who is a wonderful angel. Thank you so much for your support.

8 Aunty Irene for your warm heart and patience and for teaching me the ways of the Nonyas.

9 Tina for making a special launch party possible.

10 Rachel for your support and prayers.

11 Margaret for your impeccable editing.

12 Shing for your invaluable design advice.

13 Richard for your legal advice.

14 Last but not least, I thank the Lord for His blessings.

METHOD

1 Start with an idea. Assemble a great team including a publisher and photographer.

2 Add in generous amounts of passion, some sound legal advice and a dash of risk.

3 Combine well then set aside. After several months, a manuscript and photographs will emerge.

4 Edit the text thoroughly several times.

5 Layout the text and photographs. Add extra sections and garnish with fine details.

6 Serve warm with family and friends.

soups

Pong Tauhu Soup

A soup with pork and prawn meatballs and shredded bamboo shoots

This soup was traditionally served as a religious offering. Since it is easy to prepare and very tasty, it is also frequently served at simple home meals. A soup that is well made should have a layer of brownish-orange coloured oil which indicates that the prawn shells have been properly fried. Use fresh bamboo shoots, if available. For a healthier version of this dish, use lean pork.

INGREDIENTS

MEATBALLS

3 spring onions (scallions)

10 cloves garlic *(bawang putih)*

600 g (3 pieces) firm tofu *(taukua)*

300 g prawns (shrimps)

300 g minced pork

1/2 tbsp dark soy sauce

1/2 tbsp salt

1 tsp pepper

1 egg

SOUP STOCK

300 g cooked bamboo shoots *(rebung)*

80 g belly pork

2 l water

9 tbsp oil

1 tsp salted soy beans *(taucheo)*

1 1/2 tsp salt

PREPARATION

1 Finely slice the spring onions. Peel and finely mince the garlic.

2 Using a mortar and pestle, pound then squeeze the firm tofu dry. (Use a muslin bag, if necessary).

3 Shell and devein the prawns. Set aside the shells and roughly mince the meat.

4 Slice the bamboo shoots into fine 2.5 cm long strips. (Use only the turgid portion for canned bamboo shoots). Squeeze dry.

METHOD

1 To prepare the stock, place the belly pork and water in a large pot. Bring to the boil then simmer for 10 min. Skim off and discard the impurities that rise to the surface.

2 Remove the pork then slice into 2.5 cm strips.

3 Heat a wok over a high flame until it smokes. Add 6 tbsp oil. Lower the flame, then stir-fry the garlic until light golden brown. Strain the garlic and oil through a sieve into a small bowl.

4 To prepare the meatball mixture, knead together the pounded tofu, minced prawns, fried garlic and the remaining ingredients for the meatballs in a bowl.

5 Dip your fingers in some garlic oil then shape the meatball mixture into 2.5 cm size balls. (This will result in meatballs with a smooth texture). Lay them on a tray and set aside.

6 Heat the wok over a high flame until it smokes. Add the remaining oil. Stir-fry the prawn shells until crisp. Remove then pound the shells in a mortar and pestle.

7 In a bowl, add the pork stock to the pounded shells then pass it through a sieve back into the large pot. Discard the shells.

8 Heat the wok over a medium flame. Add 2 tbsp of the garlic-flavoured oil. Add the salted soy beans then sprinkle some water (to prevent it from burning).

9 Add the belly pork and stir-fry for 2 min. Add the bamboo shoots and continue frying for 3 min. Remove and add to the stock. Bring the stock to the boil.

10 Roll the meatballs in the remaining garlic-flavoured oil then drop them in the boiling stock. Simmer for 5–10 min. Add salt to taste.

Hee Peow Soup

A clear soup served with three types of meatballs, fish bladder, pork tripe and cabbage

This Straits Chinese soup was traditionally served only during weddings and birthdays. It is a laborious dish to cook, since each of the meatballs is prepared separately and hand-rolled. Some Nonyas now use ready-made fish paste, fish balls and prawn balls from the wet market. If using ready-made ingredients, the trick is to buy the freshest and best quality ingredients.

INGREDIENTS
160 g fried fish bladder/maw
   (hee peow)
1 pork tripe
1.2 kg cabbage

STOCK
1.2 kg pork or pork bones
6 l water

MEATBALLS
1.2 kg finely minced fish
300 g prawns (shrimps)
30 g minced pork fat (optional)
160 g minced pork
water
pepper
salt
2 eggs
$1/4$ tsp yellow food colouring
   (optional)

---

* How to prepare pork tripe
- Turn the tripe inside out.
- Use a spoon to scrape off any residue/slime.
- Rub with salt then rinse with cold running water until the lining is free of slime.
- Cook in boiling water for 30 min until tender.
- Remove and plunge in cold running water.

PREPARATION
1 Soak the fried fish bladder in water. Rinse then cut into pieces.
2 Prepare the pork tripe.*
3 Shell, devein then finely mince the prawns. (Freeze the shells for use in other recipes).
4 Separate the egg yolks and whites.
5 Slice the cabbage.

METHOD
Stock
1 To make the stock, bring the pork bones and cold water to the boil then simmer for at least 30 min, if not more. Skim off and discard the impurities that rise to the surface. Strain the stock into a large pot and discard the bones.

Fish Balls
1 In a bowl, combine half the minced fish with a dash of pepper. Beat well, then gradually add 350 ml of water while stirring continuously. Beat until the mixture is smooth, then add 1 tbsp salt.
2 Form the fish balls by scooping the minced fish mixture with one hand and squeezing it between your index finger and thumb. With a spoon in the other hand, scoop the mixture into a ball then drop it into a basin of salted water. Leave the fish balls aside for 1 hr to set, then drain. Discard the water.
3 Bring the stock to the boil then drop the fish balls in. The fish balls will rise to the surface when cooked (about 3–4 min). Drain then set aside.

Prawn Balls
1 Combine half of the remaining minced fish with the minced prawns, minced pork fat (optional), egg yolks, a dash of pepper, salt and yellow food colouring. Mix well, then take 1 rounded tbsp of the mixture and roll it into a ball. Place on a greased tray.
2 Steam for about 5 min.

Pork and Fish Balls
1 Combine the remaining minced fish, minced pork, a dash of pepper and egg whites. Shape the mixture into 2.5 cm balls. Place on a greased tray.
2 Steam for about 5 min.

Serving
1 Just before serving, bring the stock to the boil then add the tripe, fish bladder, cabbage and meatballs. Simmer for 10 min before serving.
2 Add salt to taste.

Bawan Kepiting Soup

A soup with meatballs and bamboo shoots

This soup was traditionally served at weddings. Use fresh prepared crabmeat to lighten the work. For a healthier version, use lean minced pork.

INGREDIENTS

MEATBALLS

200 g crabmeat
    (from 1.2 kg crabs)

300 g minced pork

300 g minced fish

50 g cooked bamboo shoots
    (rebung)

5 cloves garlic *(bawang putih)*

1 egg

1 tsp salt

1 tsp light soy sauce

3 tbsp oil

STOCK

300 g cooked bamboo shoots
    (rebung)

2.3 l water

$^1/_2$ tsp sugar

2 tsp salt

PREPARATION

1 In a steamer, bring some water to the boil then steam the crabs for about 10 min, depending on the size of the crabs. Set aside the crabs to cool before removing the meat.

2 Finely shred 50 g of bamboo shoots (for the meatballs). Shred the remaining 300 g of bamboo shoots (for the stock).

3 Peel and finely mince the garlic.

4 Combine the finely shredded bamboo shoots, crabmeat and remaining ingredients for the meatball mixture.

METHOD

1 Heat a wok over a high flame until it smokes. Add the oil. Lower the flame, then stir-fry the garlic until light golden brown. Remove the garlic, drain and add it to the meatball mixture. Mix well.

2 Shape the mixture into 2.5 cm balls. Place on a greased tray. Set aside.

3 Fry the 300 g of bamboo shoots for about 2 min. Remove.

4 Bring the water to the boil, then drop in the meatballs. Add the bamboo shoots to the soup, then simmer for 10 min.

5 Add sugar and salt to taste.

Kiam Chai Soup (Itik Tim)

Duck and preserved cabbage in a pork soup

A Nonya classic, this soup is commonly served in restaurants and homes. It is easy to make although the use of duck and pork does result in an oily soup. I would suggest trimming excess fat from the duck, or for a healthier version, remove the skin of the duck entirely and use lean pork.

INGREDIENTS

1 whole duck

600 g salted cabbage *(kiam chai)*

1 fresh tamarind *(asam)* pod

1 thumb size knob galangal
   (lengkuas)

600 g pork or pork bones

4.5 l water

1 tbsp brandy

salt

PREPARATION

1 Rub the duck with some brandy, then cut into pieces and rinse.

2 Soak the salted cabbage in water for 10 min. Discard the water. (Do not soak too long as the cabbage will lose its saltiness).

3 Remove the hard outer shell of the tamarind pod.

4 Peel then bruise the galangal.

METHOD

1 Rinse then place the pork or pork bones in a large pot of water. Bring to the boil then simmer for 10 min. Skim off and discard the impurities that surface.

2 Add the duck and bring to the boil again. Continue to skim off impurities and excess oil that surfaces.

3 Add the salted cabbage, fresh tamarind, galangal and remaining brandy. Simmer until the duck is tender (about 30 min or more). Add salt to taste.

salads

vegetables

pickles

Sambal Kim Chiam

A salad of dried lily buds, bilimbi fruit, cucumber and prawns served with a coconut dressing

INGREDIENTS

80 g dried lily buds *(kim chiam)*

160 g medium-sized prawns (shrimps)

1 cucumber

8 bilimbi fruit *(belimbing asam)*

1 red chilli

250 g grated coconut

100 ml water

¹/₄ tsp salt

REMPAH

2 red chillies

1 tbsp prawn (shrimp) paste *(belacan)*

3 tbsp kalamansi lime *(limau kesturi)* juice or 1 tbsp lemon juice

2 tbsp sugar

¹/₄ tsp salt

PREPARATION

1 Wash then blanch the dried lily buds in boiling water. Squeeze dry.

2 Boil, shell then devein the prawns. (Freeze the shells for use in other recipes).

3 Peel and cut the cucumber in half lengthwise, then deseed and shred.

4 Wash and cut the bilimbi in half, then finely slice.

5 Deseed then shred 1 red chilli. Soak in cold water.

6 Prepare the coconut cream. (See page 185). Simmer the coconut cream and salt over a low fire until it has thickened slightly.

7 To make the *rempah*, deseed then roughly chop the 2 red chillies. Wrap the prawn paste in aluminium foil then toast. Pound/blend the chopped chillies and toasted prawn paste together. Add the lime/lemon juice, sugar and salt last.

METHOD

1 Mix the dried lily buds, *rempah* and half the thickened coconut cream together. Place on a serving plate and top with the cucumber, bilimbi and prawns. Pour the remaining coconut cream over then garnish with the shredded chilli.

Jantung Pisang

A salad of banana bud, cucumber and prawns in coconut cream

Jantung Pisang was traditionally served during weddings. This dish is no longer found on the menus of Nonya restaurants and is seldom served in most Nonya homes because the method of preparing the banana bud has been lost. It is difficult to locate banana buds in Singapore, although wet markets such as the ones at Tekka and Geylang Serai still sell them.

INGREDIENTS

2 large banana buds
  (jantung pisang)

300 g small prawns (shrimps)

1 cucumber

10 shallots *(bawang merah)*

10 bilimbi fruit *(belimbing asam)*

250 g grated coconut

100 ml water

3 tbsp sugar

2 tsp salt

REMPAH

2 tbsp prawn (shrimp) paste
  (belacan)

4 red chillies

4 tbsp kalamansi lime *(limau
  kesturi)* juice

PREPARATION

1 Remove and discard the hard fibrous purple outer layers of the banana buds. Keep only the soft white inner layers, the white banana flowers and petals. Slice the soft layers. Discard the hard centre. (Keep the sliced banana buds fully immersed in water to prevent discolouring).

2 Blanch the sliced banana buds in hot water, then rinse and drain well.

3 Blanch and devein the prawns.

4 Peel and cut the cucumber in half lengthwise, then deseed and shred.

5 Peel then finely slice the shallots. Slice the bilimbi.

6 Prepare the coconut cream. (See page 185). Simmer the coconut cream and salt over a low fire until it has thickened slightly.

7 To prepare the *rempah*, deseed then roughly chop the chillies. Pound/blend the chillies and prawn paste, adding the lime juice last.

METHOD

1 Place the banana buds, shallots, bilimbi and cucumber on a serving dish. Garnish with prawns and then chill.

2 Add the *rempah* and sugar to the thickened coconut cream. Mix well and allow to cool before pouring over the vegetables.

3 Serve slightly chilled.

He Sei

Salad served with raw fish and a spicy sauce

The highlight of this dish is the wolf herring *(ikan parang)*. It is not easy to locate although it is available in some wet markets. Ensure that the fish is fresh since it is eaten raw. Wolf herring has many bones, so use your fingers to remove the bones before freezing.

INGREDIENTS

300 g fish, preferably wolf herring *(ikan parang)*

1 cucumber

2 heads local lettuce

10 sprigs Chinese celery

1 white turnip *(lobak)*

1 small piece salted radish *(chai po)*

SAUCE

1 thumb size knob galangal *(lengkuas)*

3 tbsp chilli sauce

3 tbsp vinegar

3 tbsp kalamansi lime *(limau kesturi)* juice

1 tbsp sugar

120 ml plum jam *(tim mui)*

60 g peanuts, roasted and ground

3 tbsp toasted white sesame seeds

$1/2$ tbsp salt

PREPARATION

1 Cut the fish lengthwise then rinse in salted water. Pat dry, then freeze until it is firm. With a very sharp knife, slice the fish as thinly as possible. Set aside to allow it to defrost.

2 Rinse then cut the cucumber in half lengthwise. Slice diagonally.

3 Rinse, pat dry then tear the lettuce into small pieces.

4 Rinse, pat dry then slice the Chinese celery.

5 Peel then shred the white turnip.

6 Shred or mince the salted radish.

7 Prepare the sauce. Peel and grate the galangal, then mix all the ingredients for the sauce together.

METHOD

1 Arrange the vegetables on a serving platter in the following order: cucumber, lettuce, Chinese celery, white turnip and salted radish. Spread the fish slices over the vegetables. Pour the sauce over the salad before serving.

Chap Chai

Stewed vegetables with prawns and pork in a soy bean sauce

Nonya Chap Chai is an adaptation of the Chinese vegetarian dish. The Nonya dish includes meat and *rempah*. It is relatively easy to make, and since most of the ingredients are dried or preserved, they can be stored for months and used when required. For a healthier vegetarian version, exclude the prawns and belly pork.

INGREDIENTS

40 g dried lily buds *(kim chiam)*

10 g cloud/wood ear fungus
   (boh jee)

10 g dried Chinese mushrooms

4 pieces dried sweet tofu slices
   (tiam taukee)

2 sticks dried yellow tofu skin
   (taukee)

10 g glass noodles *(tunghoon)*

250 g cabbage

2 tbsp salted soy beans
   (taucheo)

320 g medium-sized prawns
   (shrimps)

320 g belly pork

6 tbsp oil

sugar

salt

REMPAH

4 candlenuts *(buah keras)*

20 shallots *(bawang merah)*

2 red chillies

STOCK

prawn shells

1 l water

PREPARATION

1 Soak the dried lily buds, cloud/wood ear fungus, dried Chinese mushrooms, dried tofu and glass noodles in hot water.

2 Rinse and cut the cabbage into 2.5 cm squares.

3 Pound the salted soy beans.

4 Shell and devein the prawns. Reserve the shells for the stock.

5 Cut the belly pork into small strips.

6 Prepare the stock. Pound the prawn shells then add to the water.

7 Prepare the *rempah*. Peel and roughly chop the shallots and chillies. Pound/blend together with the candlenuts.

METHOD

1 Heat a wok over a high flame until it smokes. Add the oil. Stir-fry the *rempah*. Sprinkle some water, then add the salted soy beans.

2 Add the prawns and pork. Sprinkle some water into the wok again. Drain then add all the soaked ingredients and cabbage.

3 Strain and pour the prawn stock into the wok.

4 Bring to the boil then simmer for 20 min. Add sugar and salt to taste.

Penang Achar

Penang-style pickled vegetables

Achar was traditionally served in *kum chings* such as the one shown in this photo. This *achar* recipe is my family's favourite. We keep small jars of it in the fridge and serve it at every meal. *Achar* keeps well in the fridge for months. In the olden days, my aunts would make large batches then bottle them and give them away as gifts. *Achar* is considered a key side dish in every Nonya meal, along with *sambal belacan*.

INGREDIENTS

2.4 kg cucumbers
160 g French beans
160 g long beans
160 g cabbage
600 g carrots
600 g cauliflower
10 red chillies
10 green chillies
300 g garlic *(bawang putih)*
160 g white sesame seeds
300 g peanuts, roasted and ground
280 ml vinegar
150 g sugar
1¹/₂ tbsp salt
180 ml oil

REMPAH

20 dried chillies or 4 tbsp freshly pounded red chillies
2 thumb size knobs turmeric *(kunyit)* or 2 tbsp turmeric powder

PREPARATION

1. If dried chillies are used for the *rempah*, soak in hot water.
2. Rinse then cut the cucumber in half lengthwise. Using a spoon, scrape away the seeds. Cut away the ends, then slice into 2.5 cm long strips. Mix with 1 tbsp salt to help draw out the water. Place the cucumbers in a colander with a heavy object to press them down. Allow the water to drain.
3. Rinse then cut the French beans and long beans into 2.5 cm long strips.
4. Cut the cabbage into 2.5 cm wide strips.
5. Peel then cut the carrots into 2.5 cm long strips.
6. Cut the cauliflower into small pieces/florettes.
7. Slit the red and green chillies lengthwise, then deseed, if preferred.
8. Peel then pound the garlic. Place in muslin bag then squeeze dry.
9. Prepare the *rempah*. Deseed then roughly chop the soaked dried or fresh chillies. Peel the turmeric. Pound/blend the chillies and turmeric together.

METHOD

1. Bring the vinegar to the boil. Blanch all of the vegetables (except the chillies) in the vinegar separately. (The vinegar must be at boiling point each time. This will ensure that the vegetables are cooked and remain crunchy, not soft).
2. Remove and drain any excess vinegar. Spread the vegetables on a large tray to cool and allow excess water to evaporate. (If necessary, squeeze the vegetables in a muslin bag to remove any excess liquid).
3. Heat a wok over a high flame until it smokes. Add the oil. Lower the fire then stir-fry the sesame seeds until golden brown. Remove and drain. Allow to cool, then pound/blend.
4. Over a medium flame, reheat the oil. Stir-fry the garlic until golden brown. Remove and drain.
5. Stir-fry the *rempah* until fragrant. Turn off the flame, then add the salt. Set the *rempah* aside to cool.
6. In a large bowl, mix the vegetables and chillies. Add the fried *rempah*, fried garlic, pounded sesame seeds, ground peanuts and sugar to taste.
7. Cover then set aside overnight for the flavours to infuse. Store in clean, airtight, glass jars in the refrigerator.

Achar with Rempah

Pickled vegetables with stuffed chillies

This *achar* recipe requires a little more work since it has two types of *rempah* and includes stuffed chillies. It is very similar to Penang Achar but it includes peanut candy and ginger and excludes French beans and long beans. The cooking methodology is also slightly different.

INGREDIENTS

2.4 kg cucumbers

600 g cauliflower

300 g cabbage

160 g carrots

3 tbsp white sesame seeds

300 g peanut candy *(gula kacang)*

1 thumb size knob ginger *(halia)*

150 ml oil

VINEGAR MIXTURE

(for blanching)

700 ml vinegar

350 ml water

2 tbsp sugar

1 tbsp salt

REMPAH

2 thumb size knobs turmeric
　(kunyit)

10 shallots *(bawang merah)*

5 candlenuts *(buah keras)*

20 dried chillies

VINEGAR MIXTURE

(for the *rempah*)

350 ml vinegar

350 ml water

300 g sugar

PREPARATION

1　Soak the dried chillies for the *rempah* in hot water.

2　Rinse then cut the cucumber in half lengthwise. Using a spoon, scrap away the seeds. Cut away the ends, then slice into 2.5 cm long strips. Mix with 1 tbsp salt to help draw out the water. Place the cucumbers in a colander with a heavy object to press them down. Allow the water to drain.

3　Cut the cauliflower into small pieces/florettes.

4　Cut the cabbage into 2.5 cm wide strips.

5　Peel then cut the carrots into 2.5 cm long strips.

6　Toast or fry the sesame seeds until light golden brown.

7　Finely pound the peanut candy.

8　Peel then shred the ginger.

9　Prepare the *rempah*. Deseed then roughly chop the soaked dried chillies. Peel then roughly chop the turmeric and shallots. Pound/blend all the *rempah* ingredients together.

METHOD

1　Combine the ingredients for the vinegar mixture for blanching. Bring to the boil. Blanch each of the vegetables separately. (The vinegar must be at boiling point each time. This will ensure that the vegetables are cooked and remain crunchy, not soft).

2　Remove and drain any excess vinegar. Spread the vegetables on a large tray to cool and allow excess water to evaporate.

3　Heat a wok over a high flame until it smokes. Add the oil. Stir-fry the ginger over a medium flame until light golden brown. Remove the ginger and add the *rempah*. Stir-fry for a few minutes until fragrant. Add the vinegar mixture for the *rempah*. Mix well. Turn off the flame then allow the oil from the *rempah* to surface.

4　Reheat the wok then separately stir-fry each of the vegetables in the *rempah*. Set aside to cool.

5　Prepare the Achar Chillies. (See page 36).

6　In a large bowl, combine the vegetables, stuffed chillies, fried ginger and peanut candy. Pour the remaining *rempah* over. Mix well.

7　Cover then set aside overnight for the flavours to infuse. Store in clean, airtight, glass jars in the refrigerator.

Achar Chillies (Stuffed Chillies)

Chillies stuffed with fried dried prawns

Traditionally, the chillies were soaked in a solution of slaked lime or ground seashells *(kapur)* to make the chillies crunchy. I find it sufficient to simply blanch the chillies in vinegar. For those who would prefer to use *kapur*, it is available at some provision stores and wet markets.

INGREDIENTS

10 red chillies

10 green chillies

$^1/_2$ tsp slaked lime *(kapur)* (optional)

100 g dried prawns (shrimps) *(udang kering)*

4 tbsp green papaya

$^1/_4$ tsp salt

1 tbsp sugar

5 tbsp oil

REMPAH

5 shallots *(bawang merah)*

2 candlenuts *(buah keras)*

$^1/_2$ tsp prawn (shrimp) paste *(belacan)*

PREPARATION

1 Make a slit lengthwise along the red and green chillies then deseed (if preferred).

2 Soak in a solution of water and slaked lime for 30 min. Rinse and drain well (optional).

3 Pound/blend the dried prawns.

4 Grate the green papaya, add salt, then sun to dry.

5 Prepare the *rempah*. Peel then roughly chop the shallots. Pound/blend together with the candlenuts and prawn paste.

METHOD

1 Heat a wok over a high flame until it smokes. Add the oil. Stir-fry the *rempah* for 3–4 min, then add the dried prawns. Turn off the flame then stir in the sugar, salt and papaya. Leave to cool.

2 If the chillies have not been soaked in *kapur*, blanch the chillies in the same vinegar solution as the vegetables in Achar with Rempah (see page 34). Remove and drain well. Stuff with the cooled *rempah* and dried prawns mixture.

3 Add the chillies to the other vegetables in the Achar with Rempah dish.

seafood

Garam Asam

A dish of prawns or fish served in a tangy sour sauce

The Malay name of this dish is literally 'irresistibly sour'. The sour flavour of this dish whets the appetite without being too strong. It is well balanced with the other ingredients and is a perfect contrast to the sweetness of the prawns or fish. Cook this dish with tiger or king-sized prawns, Spanish mackerel *(ikan tenggiri)*, red snapper or sea bass.

INGREDIENTS

600 g prawns (shrimps) or fish

2 rounded tbsp tamarind *(asam)* pulp

850 ml water

120 ml oil

2 tbsp sugar

2 tbsp salt

REMPAH

10 slices galangal *(lengkuas)*

$^1/_2$ thumb size knob turmeric *(kunyit)*

20 shallots *(bawang merah)*

4 red chillies

4 candlenuts *(buah keras)*

$^1/_2$ tbsp prawn (shrimp) paste *(belacan)*

1 stalk lemon grass *(serai)*

PREPARATION

1 Prepare the prawns or fish. (If prawns are used, trim off the sharp feelers and legs then rinse).

2 Prepare the tamarind marinade. (See page 185).

3 Prepare the *rempah*. Peel the galangal, turmeric, shallots and lemon grass. Coarsely pound/blend all the *rempah* ingredients, then add the bruised lemon grass (use white portion only) last.

METHOD

1 Heat a wok over a high flame until it smokes. Add the oil. Stir-fry the *rempah* for 2 min. Lower the flame, then fry for another 2 min. Add about 3 tbsp tamarind marinade and continue frying for 2 min.

2 Over a high flame, add the remaining tamarind marinade, sugar and salt. Bring to the boil then add the prawns or fish. Bring to the boil again. Simmer uncovered for 5 min. Serve.

Kuah Ladah

Stingray served in a tamarind and pepper gravy

The highlight of this dish is the stingray. If it is not available, use pomfret.

INGREDIENTS

600 g fish, preferably stingray
 (ikan pari)

300 g eggplant (aubergine/
 brinjal)

4 rounded tbsp tamarind *(asam)*
 pulp

850 ml water

5 tbsp oil

1 1/2 tbsp sugar

1 tbsp salt

REMPAH

1 1/2 tbsp peppercorns or 1 tsp
 pepper

10 slices galangal *(lengkuas)*

1/2 thumb size knob turmeric
 (kunyit)

15 shallots *(bawang merah)*

2 cloves garlic *(bawang putih)*

4 candlenuts *(buah keras)*

1 1/2 tbsp prawn (shrimp) paste
 (belacan)

PREPARATION

1 Rinse and cut the fish into pieces.

2 Slice the eggplant into thick pieces.

3 Prepare the tamarind marinade. (See page 185).

4 Prepare the *rempah*. Peel and roughly chop the galangal, turmeric, shallots and garlic. Pound/blend all the *rempah* ingredients together.

METHOD

1 Heat a wok over a high flame until it smokes. Add the oil. Stir-fry the *rempah* for 2 min. Sprinkle in about 2 tbsp tamarind marinade, then continue to stir-fry for 3 min.

2 Add the eggplant and continue to stir-fry. Add the remaining tamarind marinade.

3 Bring to the boil then add the fish. Leave to simmer until the fish is cooked and tender (about 5–10 min). Add sugar and salt to taste.

Ikan Pedas

Fish braised in a spicy tamarind gravy

The Malay name of this dish translates literally into 'spicy fish'. This gravy goes well with fish, prawns (shrimps), squid or crabs.

INGREDIENTS

600 g seafood

2 fresh tamarind *(asam)* pods

2 rounded tbsp tamarind *(asam)* pulp

850 ml water

1 tbsp oil (optional)

2 tbsp sugar

$^3/_4$ tbsp salt

REMPAH

10 slices galangal *(lengkuas)*

$^1/_2$ thumb size knob turmeric *(kunyit)*

30 shallots *(bawang merah)*

4 red chillies

1 tbsp prawn (shrimp) paste *(belacan)*

PREPARATION

1 Prepare the seafood. (If prawns are used, trim off the sharp feelers and legs then rinse).

2 Remove the hard outer shell of the tamarind pod.

3 Prepare the tamarind marinade. (See page 185).

4 Pepare the *rempah*. Peel the galangal, turmeric and shallots. Deseed (if preferred) then roughly chop the chillies. Very finely pound/blend the galangal and turmeric, then add and coarsely pound/blend the shallots, chillies and prawn paste.

METHOD

1 In a large pot, combine the *rempah*, tamarind marinade and fresh tamarind.

2 Bring to the boil and add the seafood and the oil (optional). Simmer until the meat is cooked (about 3–7 min, depending on the seafood used).

3 Add sugar and salt to taste.

Asam Putih

Seafood in a tamarind gravy

The Malay name of this dish literally translates to 'sour white' because unlike other tamarind-based gravy dishes which are sour and yellow, this dish is sour, but not yellow in colour. This dish is healthy and very simple to prepare. Fresh prawns, squid or a small pomfret work well with this gravy.

INGREDIENTS

300 g seafood

1 onion

1 stalk lemon grass (serai)

2 red chillies

6 green chillies

$1^1/_2$ rounded tbsp tamarind (asam) pulp

570 ml water

$^1/_2$ tbsp prawn (shrimp) paste (belacan)

$2^1/_2$ tbsp sugar

$1^1/_2$ tbsp salt

PREPARATION

1 Prepare the seafood. (If prawns are used, trim off the sharp feelers and legs then rinse).

2 Peel then slice the onion. Peel then bruise the lemon grass (use white portion only).

3 Slit the red and green chillies lengthwise and deseed, if preferred.

4 Prepare the tamarind marinade. (See page 185).

METHOD

1 Bring all the ingredients (except the seafood) to the boil. Simmer for 5 min to allow the gravy to thicken. Add the seafood then simmer for another 3–5 min until cooked.

Udang Pedas Nanas

Prawns and pineapple in a spicy gravy

This dish is one of my favourites. It is typically prepared using prawns, however, fish can also be used. The key is to use fresh seafood and a sweet but not over-ripe pineapple.

INGREDIENTS

600 g prawns (shrimps) or fish

1 small pineapple *(nanas)*

1 l water

2 tbsp sugar

1 tbsp salt

REMPAH

15 slices galangal *(lengkuas)*

$^1/_2$ thumb size knob turmeric *(kunyit)*

20 shallots *(bawang merah)*

4 red chillies

$1^1/_2$ tbsp prawn (shrimp) paste *(belacan)*

PREPARATION

1 Prepare the prawns or fish. (If prawns are used, trim off the sharp feelers and legs then rinse. Alternatively, shell them entirely).

2 Peel and cut the pineapple into chunks.

3 Prepare the *rempah*. Peel the galangal, turmeric and shallots. Roughly chop the chillies. Finely pound/blend together with the prawn paste.

METHOD

1 Bring the *rempah*, pineapple and water to the boil. Simmer uncovered for 5–10 min to thicken the gravy.

2 Add the prawns or fish. Simmer for about 3–5 min until the meat is cooked. Add sugar and salt to taste.

Ikan Asam Surani

Fish served in a spicy tamarind and turmeric gravy

If herring *(ikan terubuk)* is not available, alternatives include Spanish mackerel *(ikan tenggiri)*, sea bass and red snapper.

INGREDIENTS

600 g fish, preferably herring
   (ikan terubuk)

12 shallots *(bawang merah)*

6 cloves garlic *(bawang putih)*

1 stalk lemon grass *(serai)*

6 red chillies

6 rounded tbsp tamarind *(asam)*
   pulp

850 ml water

6 tbsp oil

6 tbsp sugar

1 tbsp salt

REMPAH

1 thumb size knob turmeric
   (kunyit)

1 1/2 tbsp prawn (shrimp)
   paste *(belacan)*

PREPARATION

1 Rinse then cut the fish into pieces.

2 Peel then slice the shallots and garlic.

3 Peel then bruise the lemon grass (use white portion only). Slice the chillies.

4 Prepare the tamarind marinade. (See page 185).

5 Prepare the *rempah*. Peel then roughly chop the turmeric. Pound/blend together with the prawn paste.

METHOD

1 Heat a wok over a high flame until it smokes. Add the oil. Lower the flame, add the shallots then garlic. Stir-fry until golden brown. Remove and drain.

2 Stir-fry the lemon grass and chillies. Remove and drain.

3 Add the *rempah*, sprinkle in some water then stir-fry. Over a high flame, add the tamarind marinade and bring to the boil. Add the fried ingredients and fish.

4 Lower to a simmer and cook for a further 3–5 min (be careful not to overcook the fish). Add sugar and salt to taste. Garnish with sliced chillies.

Penang Fish/Prawn Gulai

Fish or prawns and okra or eggplants served in a spicy gravy, lightly flavoured with laksa leaves

Gulai is the Peranakan term for curry. It is typically seafood or meat with a vegetable or fruit in a spicy coconut gravy. This dish can be served in a combination of fish or prawns and okra and eggplant (see inset picture of Prawn Gulai). Any type of meaty white fish such as sea bass, red snapper, Spanish mackerel *(ikan tenggiri)* or threadfin *(ikan kurau)*, or tiger prawns can be used.

INGREDIENTS

600 g fish or prawns (shrimps)

300 g okra (ladies' fingers) or eggplant (aubergine/brinjal)

4 stalks laksa leaves *(daun kesum)*

1¹/₂ rounded tbsp tamarind *(asam)* pulp

700 ml water

6 tbsp oil

3 tbsp sugar

2 tsp salt

REMPAH

2 stalks lemon grass *(serai)*

¹/₂ thumb size knob turmeric *(kunyit)*

20 dried chillies

2 cloves garlic *(bawang putih)*

20 shallots *(bawang merah)*

¹/₂ tbsp prawn (shrimp) paste *(belacan)*

PREPARATION

1 Soak the dried chillies for the *rempah* in hot water.

2 Prepare the fish or prawns. (If prawns are used, trim off the sharp feelers and legs then rinse).

3 Rinse and cut the okra or eggplant into pieces.

4 Rinse and pluck the laksa leaves from the stems. Discard the stems.

5 Prepare the tamarind marinade. (See page 185).

6 Prepare the *rempah*. Deseed then roughly chop the soaked dried chillies. Peel the lemon grass, turmeric, garlic and shallots. Roughly chop the lemon grass (use white portion only). Pound/blend all the *rempah* ingredients together.

METHOD

1 Heat a wok over a high flame until it smokes. Add the oil. Lower the flame then add the *rempah*. Stir-fry for 3 min.

2 Add the sugar and salt. Stir-fry for another 2 min. Add the tamarind marinade and bring to the boil. Add the fish or prawns, vegetables and laksa leaves. Simmer for 5–8 min.

Gulai Ikan

Fish and bamboo shoots served in a curry gravy

Any type of meaty white fish such as sea bass, red snapper, Spanish mackerel *(ikan tenggiri)* or threadfin *(ikan kurau),* or prawns can be used in this recipe.

INGREDIENTS

600 g fish or prawns

160 g cooked bamboo shoots *(rebung)*

1 fresh tamarind *(asam)* pod or 1¹/₂ rounded tbsp tamarind *(asam)* pulp and 6 tbsp water

500 g grated coconut

700 ml water

6 tbsp oil

1 tbsp sugar

¹/₂ tbsp salt

REMPAH

6 slices galangal *(lengkuas)*

¹/₂ thumb size knob turmeric *(kunyit)*

4 slices ginger *(halia)*

10 shallots *(bawang merah)*

1 clove garlic *(bawang putih)*

10 red chillies or 1 tbsp pounded chillies

¹/₂ tbsp prawn (shrimp) paste *(belacan)*

¹/₂ tsp cumin *(jintan putih)* powder

2 tsp coriander *(ketumbar)* powder

1 stalk lemon grass *(serai)*

PREPARATION

1 Prepare the fish or prawns. (If prawns are used, trim off the sharp feelers and legs then rinse).

2 Slice the bamboo shoots.

3 Prepare the tamarind marinade. (See page 185).

4 Prepare the coconut milk. (See page 185).

5 Prepare the *rempah*. Peel the galangal, turmeric, ginger, shallots and garlic then roughly chop together with the chillies (deseed, if preferred). Pound/blend together with the prawn paste, cumin powder and coriander powder. Add the peeled and bruised lemon grass (use white portion only) last.

METHOD

1 Heat a wok over a high flame until it smokes. Add the oil. Stir-fry the *rempah* for 1 min. Add 5 tbsp coconut milk and simmer for a few min.

2 Add the bamboo shoots, remaining coconut milk and tamarind marinade.

3 Bring to the boil then add the fish. Simmer for 5–10 min. Add sugar and salt to taste.

Gulai Udang

Prawns in a thin curry gravy

INGREDIENTS

600 g prawns (shrimps)

1 fresh tamarind (asam) pod

6 green chillies

10 shallots (bawang merah)

1 stalk lemon grass (serai)

6 tbsp oil

500 g grated coconut

850 ml water

1 tsp sugar

2 tsp salt

REMPAH

10 dried chillies

4 slices galangal (lengkuas)

^{1}/$_4$ thumb size knob turmeric (kunyit)

2 slices ginger (halia)

2 cloves garlic (bawang putih)

1 tsp prawn (shrimp) paste (belacan)

2 tsp coriander (ketumbar) powder

^{1}/$_2$ tsp cumin (jintan putih) powder

PREPARATION

1   Soak the dried chillies for the *rempah* in hot water.

2   Shell and devein the prawns. (Freeze the shells for use in other recipes).

3   Remove the hard outer shell of the tamarind pod.

4   Slit the green chillies lengthwise and deseed, if preferred.

5   Peel and slice the shallots.

6   Peel then bruise the lemon grass (use white portion only).

7   Prepare the *rempah*. Deseed then roughly chop the soaked dried chillies. Peel and roughly chop the galangal, turmeric, ginger and garlic. Pound/blend together with the prawn paste. Add the coriander powder and cumin powder last.

8   Prepare the coconut milk. (See page 185).

METHOD

1   Heat a wok over a high flame until it smokes. Add the oil. Lower the flame then stir-fry the shallots until light golden brown. Remove and drain.

2   Over a high flame, stir-fry the *rempah* and lemon grass for 1 min. Add 5 tbsp coconut milk then simmer for 2 min. Add the fried shallots, tamarind and remaining coconut milk. Bring to the boil, while stirring continually.

3   Add the prawns and green chillies then reduce to a simmer. Cook for another 5 min before adding sugar and salt to taste.

Tauhu Titek

Prawn and pork meatballs served with tofu in a gravy

INGREDIENTS

300 g or 1 pack soft tofu *(tauhu)*

80 g dried salted fish

4 sprigs Chinese celery

4 spring onions (scallions)

4 tbsp oil

MEATBALLS

160 g prawns

160 g minced pork

1 tsp light soy sauce

A dash of pepper

REMPAH

20 shallots *(bawang merah)*

2 red chillies

4 candlenuts *(buah keras)*

1 tbsp prawn (shrimp) paste
   (belacan)

STOCK

prawn shells

700 ml water

PREPARATION

1 Cut the tofu into cubes.

2 Cut the salted fish into small pieces.

3 Rinse then finely slice the Chinese celery and spring onions.

4 Shell and devein the prawns. Mince the prawns. Save the shells for the stock.

5 Combine then shape the meatball mixture into 2.5 cm size balls. Set aside.

6 To make the stock, pound the prawn shells then add water. Stir well.

7 Prepare the *rempah*. Peel and roughly chop the shallots and chillies. Pound/blend all the *rempah* ingredients together.

METHOD

1 Heat a wok over a high flame until it smokes. Add the oil. Stir-fry the *rempah* until fragrant (about 7 min).

2 Strain the prawn stock into the wok and bring to the boil. Add the meatballs then bring to the boil again.

3 Add the salted fish and tofu. Simmer for 5 min then turn off the flame. Garnish with Chinese celery and spring onions.

Sambal Belacan

A rich pungent paste served as a side dish or stuffed in seafood

Sambal belacan is considered a key side dish in every Peranakan meal, along with *achar*. It compliments many dishes with its rich pungent flavour and is used either as a stuffing (see inset picture of *ikan kembung* stuffed with *sambal belacan*) or served on the side. Although it can be used in a wide variety of dishes, grilled stingray and deep-fried fish *(ikan kuning* or *ikan kembung)* are the most common dishes where *sambal belacan* is used. Always serve dishes cooked with *sambal belacan* with a squeeze of lime juice, as it adds a refreshing sharpness to the flavour.

INGREDIENTS

1 $1/2$ tbsp prawn (shrimp) paste
   (belacan)

5 red chillies

$1/4$ tsp sugar

$1/4$ tsp salt

2 kalamansi limes *(limau kesturi)*

PREPARATION

1 Toast the prawn paste in the toaster or by dry-frying in a pan. (Wrap in foil to prevent the pungent smell from escaping).

2 Deseed the chillies, if preferred.

3 Rinse and halve the limes.

METHOD

1 Pound/blend all the ingredients together. Do not pound/blend them too finely. If a mortar and pestle are used, start by wetting the ingredients with a little water. Place the chillies on top of the prawn paste and pound. (If the chillies were not deseeded, avoid pounding the seeds unless you want a very spicy dish).

2 Add the sugar and salt and mix well. Serve in a small dish with the cut limes or store in the freezer until needed.

Dry Sambal Udang Kering

Minced dried prawns seasoned with spices

This side dish is typically eaten with rice, porridge or buttered bread. It is the perfect comfort food for a little taste of Singapore when you are far away from home. It travels and stores well in an airtight plastic bag or container. Although it is sold ready-made in jars, this homemade version is well worth the effort.

INGREDIENTS

300 g dried prawns (shrimps) *(udang kering)*

1 tbsp kalamansi lime *(limau kesturi)* or lemon juice

300 g shallots *(bawang merah)*

2 tbsp sugar

CHILLI OIL

6 red chillies

3 tbsp oil

PREPARATION

1 Rinse the dried prawns three times. Shake off the excess water then finely pound/ blend. Add the lime juice.

2 Peel then slice the shallots.

3 Pound the chillies.

METHOD

1 Heat a wok over a high flame until it smokes. Add the oil. Lower the flame then stir-fry the shallots until golden brown. Remove and drain.

2 In the same oil, stir-fry the pounded chillies. Once the oil is red, turn off the flame. Remove the pulp or strain the oil through a sieve. Discard the pulp.

3 Reheat the wok over a low flame and stir-fry the prawns in the chilli oil. Sprinkle in the sugar and continue to stir-fry until the prawns are dry and crisp.

4 Turn off the flame and add the fried shallots. Allow to cool before storing in a clean airtight plastic bag or container.

Sambal Udang Kering

Minced dried prawns seasoned with *sambal*

Although similar to Dry Sambal Udang Kering, this version is more moist and requires more ingredients.
(Suggestion: make a large batch and store for later use or pack it into small jars for giving away).

INGREDIENTS

300 g dried prawns (shrimps)
   (udang kering)

6 cloves garlic *(bawang putih)*

10 shallots *(bawang merah)*

2 stalks lemon grass *(serai)*

2 red chillies

2 green chillies

1 rounded tbsp tamarind *(asam)*
   pulp

6 tbsp water

120 ml oil

1 1/2 tbsp sugar

1/4 tsp salt

REMPAH

1/4 thumb size knob turmeric
   (kunyit)

1/2 tsp prawn (shrimp) paste
   (belacan)

PREPARATION

1 Soak the dried prawns in hot water. Drain then finely pound/blend.

2 Peel the garlic, shallots and lemon grass (use white portion only). Finely slice together with the red and green chillies (deseed, if preferred).

3 Prepare the tamarind marinade. (See page 185).

4 Prepare the *rempah*. Peel then roughly chop the turmeric. Pound/blend together with the prawn paste.

METHOD

1 Heat a wok over a high flame until it smokes. Add the oil. Lower the flame then stir-fry the garlic and shallots. Add the chillies and lemon grass and stir-fry for 1 min. Remove and drain.

2 Over a high flame, add the *rempah* and sprinkle in some water. Stir-fry for about 2 min. Reduce to a medium flame before adding the dried prawns. Stir-fry for another 2 min then add the tamarind marinade, sugar and salt.

3 Reduce to a low flame and continue stir-frying until the mixture is dry.

4 Allow to cool before storing in a clean airtight plastic bag or container.

Sambal Lengkong

Fried marinated fish flakes

If it is fried well and stored in a clean airtight container, Sambal Lengkong should remain crisp for months.

INGREDIENTS

1.2 kg fish
6 kaffir lime leaves *(daun limau purut)*
1 kg grated coconut
450 ml water
oil (for frying)

REMPAH

4 stalks lemon grass *(serai)*
4 slices galangal *(lengkuas)*
40 shallots *(bawang merah)*
2 cloves garlic *(bawang putih)*
8 red chillies
1 tsp peppercorns or pepper
12 candlenuts *(buah keras)*
1 tsp turmeric *(kunyit)* powder
6 tbsp sugar
1 tbsp salt

PREPARATION

1 Clean and cut the fish into small pieces.

2 Finely slice the kaffir lime leaves.

3 Prepare the coconut cream. (See page 185).

4 Prepare the *rempah*. Peel and roughly chop the lemon grass (use white portion only), galangal, shallots and garlic. Roughly chop the red chillies (deseed, if preferred). Pound/blend all the *rempah* ingredients together. Add the turmeric powder, sugar and salt last.

METHOD

1 In a heatproof dish, mix the *rempah* and coconut cream, then add the fish. Place in a steamer and steam until the fish is cooked (about 10–15 min).

2 Flake the fish flesh off the bones into small pieces. Discard the bones. Using your fingers, check for any remaining small bones.

3 Heat a wok over a medium flame and add some oil. Reduce to a low flame, then stir-fry the fish until crispy and dry. Remove then drain well.

4 Allow to cool before storing in a clean airtight plastic bag or container.

chicken

pork

beef

Ayam Siow

Fried chicken served in a thick tamarind sauce

This is one of my favourite Peranakan dishes and it is not difficult to prepare. It was traditionally served during Chinese New Year, since it could be made in large batches before the markets closed for the festive season. The tamarind *(asam)* and spice would preserve the chicken (during the days when there was no refrigeration), and the flavour would improve over time. According to my grandmother's cookbook, the dish is at least 150 years old.

For a healthier version, grill the chicken. I prefer to use chicken drumsticks, thighs and wings since these are the most tender parts of the chicken.

INGREDIENTS

1 whole chicken or 1 kg chicken pieces
2 tbsp oil
$^1/_2$ cucumber

MARINADE

5 rounded tbsp tamarind *(asam)* pulp
450 ml water
10 shallots *(bawang merah)*
2 tbsp coriander *(ketumbar)* powder
120 g sugar
$1^1/_2$ tbsp dark soy sauce
$1^1/_2$ tbsp vinegar
$2^1/_4$ tsp salt
$1^1/_2$ tsp pepper

PREPARATION

1 Prepare the tamarind marinade. (See page 185).
2 Peel then finely pound the shallots.
3 Toast the coriander powder in a toaster oven or by dry-frying over a low flame.
4 In a large pot, mix all the ingredients for the marinade into the tamarind marinade.
5 Cut the chicken into pieces then rinse. Place chicken in the marinade. Cover and refrigerate for 12 hours or overnight.
6 Slice the cucumber.

METHOD

1 Place the entire pot of chicken on the stove. Bring to the boil, then simmer until the meat is tender (about 30 min). Remove and drain the chicken, returning the marinade to the pot.
2 Simmer uncovered until the sauce thickens.
3 Heat a wok over a high flame until it smokes. Add the oil. Deep-fry the chicken until golden brown. Remove and drain.
4 Pour the thickened sauce over the fried chicken. Garnish with sliced cucumbers.

Ayam Buah Keluak

Chicken and pork ribs braised with *buah keluak* nuts

This is a signature dish of Nonya cuisine and also a favourite among Peranakans. Most people, however, hesitate to make this dish because it is difficult to crack open the *buah keluak* nuts to extract the meat. Originating from Indonesia, these nuts are also not easy to locate in Singapore although some wet markets do sell them. The extracted meat is also sold pre-packed at some market stalls.

To overcome the difficulty of making this dish, some people recycle the *buah keluak* shells and use the pre-packed meat for the stuffing. Alternatively, add the *buah keluak* meat on its own at the last stage of cooking, as you would the whole nuts, then simmer. The texture of the meat, however, will not be as ideal.

INGREDIENTS

20 *buah keluak* nuts

1 whole chicken or 1 kg chicken pieces

300 g pork ribs

8 rounded tbsp tamarind *(asam)* pulp

1 l water

5 tbsp sugar

5 tsp salt

120 ml oil

REMPAH

12 slices galangal *(lengkuas)*

1/2 thumb size knob turmeric *(kunyit)*

6 candlenuts *(buah keras)*

20 shallots *(bawang merah)*

10 red chillies

1 1/2 tbsp prawn (shrimp) paste *(belacan)*

1 tsp coriander *(ketumbar)* powder

1 stalk lemon grass *(serai)*

PREPARATION

1 Soak the *buah keluak* nuts for 24 hr. Scrub thoroughly with a brush. Using a cleaver or hammer, chop off the smooth area at the wider end of the nut. Reserve the shells. Using tweezers or a chopstick, remove the meat. Discard any that smell bad.

2 Pound the meat with half the amount of sugar and salt. Press the mixture back into the shells.

3 Cut the chicken and pork bones into small pieces then rinse.

4 Prepare the tamarind marinade. (See page 185).

5 Prepare the *rempah*. Peel and roughly chop the galangal, turmeric and shallots. Roughly chop the chillies (deseed, if preferred). Finely pound/blend together with the candlenuts, prawn paste and coriander powder. Add the peeled and bruised lemon grass (use white portion only) last.

METHOD

1 Heat a wok over a high flame until it smokes. Add the oil. Stir-fry the *rempah* for 2 min. Lower the flame and continue stir-frying for another 2 min.

2 Over a high flame, add the pork bones and chicken. Stir-fry until the liquid has reduced. Add the nuts and stir-fry until the oil surfaces.

3 Add the tamarind marinade and remaining sugar and salt. Simmer for at least 30 min.

Ayam Goreng

Deep-fried chicken served with a coconut gravy

INGREDIENTS

1 whole chicken or 1 kg chicken
   pieces
250 g grated coconut
280 ml water
Oil (for deep-frying)

REMPAH

4 slices galangal *(lengkuas)*
2 cloves garlic *(bawang putih)*
1 stalk lemon grass *(serai)*
1 tsp pepper
1 tsp turmeric *(kunyit)* powder
1 tsp coriander *(ketumbar)*
   powder
1 tsp sugar
1 1/2 tsp salt

PREPARATION

1 Cut the chicken into small pieces then rinse.

2 Prepare the coconut milk. (See page 185).

3 Prepare the *rempah*. Peel then roughly chop the galangal and garlic. Pound/blend together with the pepper, turmeric powder, coriander powder, sugar and salt. Add the peeled and bruised lemon grass (use white portion only) last.

METHOD

1 Mix the chicken, coconut milk and *rempah* in a wok or pot. Bring to the boil and simmer for 15 min. Remove the chicken and leave to cool. Skim off the excess fat from the gravy.

2 Bring the gravy to the boil again, then simmer uncovered for 15 min until it thickens.

3 Heat a wok over a high flame until it smokes. Add the oil. Once the oil smokes, deep-fry the chicken. Remove and drain.

4 Arrange chicken pieces on a serving plate. Serve the gravy in a separate bowl.

Ayam Sambal

Chicken served in a thick spicy coconut sauce

This is a very easy dish to prepare although it does require the preparation of a *rempah*. For a simple meal, serve with hot rice, a vegetable dish and *achar*. For a healthier version, use skinned chicken and skimmed milk.

INGREDIENTS

1 whole chicken or 1 kg chicken pieces

1 thumb size knob galangal *(lengkuas)*

1 stalk lemon grass *(serai)*

500 g grated coconut

280 ml water

1 tsp sugar

1 tsp salt

REMPAH

6 slices ginger *(halia)*

20 shallots *(bawang merah)*

6 cloves garlic *(bawang putih)*

10 red chillies or 1 tbsp pounded chillies

1 tsp prawn (shrimp) paste *(belacan)*

1 tsp coriander *(ketumbar)* powder

1 tsp cumin *(jintan putih)* powder

PREPARATION

1 Cut the chicken into large pieces then rinse.

2 Peel and bruise the galangal and lemon grass (use white portion only).

3 Prepare the coconut milk. (See page 185).

4 Prepare the *rempah*. Peel and roughly chop the ginger, shallots and garlic. Roughly chop the red chillies (deseed, if preferred). Pound/blend together with the prawn paste, adding the coriander powder and cumin powder last.

METHOD

1 Mix all the ingredients in a wok or pot. Bring to the boil. Simmer uncovered until the gravy is very thick and almost dry.

Ayam Pedas

Chicken and long beans served in a spicy gravy

INGREDIENTS

600 g chicken pieces or pork ribs

300 g long beans, cabbage or cucumber

700 ml water or chicken stock

2 tsp sugar

2 tsp salt

REMPAH

8 slices galangal *(lengkuas)*

$1/4$ thumb size knob turmeric *(kunyit)*

20 shallots *(bawang merah)*

1 stalk lemon grass *(serai)*

4 red chillies

$1^1/2$ tbsp prawn (shrimp) paste *(belacan)*

PREPARATION

1 Cut the chicken or pork ribs into pieces then rinse.

2 Slice the long beans, cabbage or cucumber into 2.5 cm pieces.

3 Prepare the *rempah*. Peel and roughly chop the galangal, turmeric, shallots and lemon grass (use white portion only). Chop the red chillies (deseed, if preferred). Finely pound/blend together with the prawn paste.

METHOD

1 Bring the *rempah* and water or chicken stock to the boil. Add the meat and simmer for 10 min.

2 Add the vegetables and continue to simmer for 3–5 min. Add sugar and salt to taste.

Ayam Kleo

Chicken served in a rich, creamy coconut gravy

The large amount of coconut milk used in this dish gives it its rich *(lemak)* taste. For a healthier version, dilute the coconut milk with more water or use chicken stock. When cooking this dish, do not use an iron wok as it will cause the gravy to discolour. Instead, use an enamel, aluminium, clay or non-stick pot.

INGREDIENTS

1 whole chicken or 1 kg chicken pieces

2 fresh tamarind *(asam)* pods

1 stalk lemon grass *(serai)*

$1/2$ thumb size knob galangal *(lengkuas)*

500 g grated coconut

850 ml water

2 tsp palm sugar *(gula Melaka)*

$1^1/2$ tsp salt

REMPAH

1 thumb size knob turmeric *(kunyit)*

12 shallots *(bawang merah)*

$1/2$ thumb size knob ginger *(halia)*

20 red chillies

$1/2$ tsp cumin *(jintan putih)* powder

2 tsp coriander *(ketumbar)* powder

PREPARATION

1 Cut the chicken into small pieces then rinse.

2 Remove the hard outer shell of the tamarind pods.

3 Peel then bruise the lemon grass (use white portion only).

4 Peel and crush the galangal.

5 Prepare the coconut milk. (See page 185).

6 Prepare the *rempah*. Peel and roughly chop the turmeric, shallots and ginger. Roughly chop the red chillies (deseed, if preferred). Very finely pound/blend together, adding the cumin powder and coriander powder last.

METHOD

1 Place all the ingredients (except the meat) in a pot. Bring to the boil, stirring constantly to prevent the mixture from splitting.

2 Add the chicken and bring to the boil again. Continue to stir. Lower to a simmer for 30 min.

Rebung Lemak

Chicken and bamboo shoots in a coconut gravy

INGREDIENTS

1 whole chicken or 1 kg chicken pieces

500 g cooked bamboo shoots (rebung)

500 g grated coconut

1 l water (200 ml for coconut cream and 800 ml for coconut milk)

120 ml oil

3/4 tbsp sugar

1 tbsp salt

REMPAH

10 slices galangal (lengkuas)

1/2 thumb size knob turmeric (kunyit)

15 shallots (bawang merah)

2 cloves garlic (bawang putih)

2 dried chillies

6 candlenuts (buah keras)

1 tbsp prawn (shrimp) paste (belacan)

1 tbsp coriander (ketumbar) powder

1 tbsp pepper

1 stalk lemon grass (serai)

PREPARATION

1 Soak the dried chillies for the *rempah* in hot water.

2 Cut the chicken into small pieces then rinse.

3 Slice the bamboo shoots.

4 Prepare the coconut milk and coconut cream. (See page 185).

5 Prepare the *rempah*. Deseed then roughly chop the soaked dried chillies. Peel and roughly chop the galangal, turmeric, shallots and garlic. Finely pound/blend together with the candlenuts, prawn paste, coriander powder and pepper. Add the peeled and bruised lemon grass (use white portion only) last.

METHOD

1 Heat a wok over a high flame until it smokes. Add the oil. Stir-fry the *rempah* for 1 min. Lower the flame and add 5 tbsp coconut milk. Stir-fry for another 2 min before adding another 5 tbsp coconut milk. Stir-fry for 2 min more.

2 Over a high flame, add and stir-fry the chicken and bamboo shoots. Pour in the remaining coconut milk and bring to the boil.

3 Add the coconut cream while stirring continuously to prevent it from splitting. Simmer for 30 min. Add sugar and salt to taste.

Satay Ayam Goreng

Boiled chicken in a spicy coconut gravy

This is a good recipe for beginners. My great great grandmother used this recipe to teach my grandmother the rudiments of Nonya cooking. It requires the skill of making a basic *rempah*, without the additional difficulty of having to fry it. For a healthier version, used skinned chicken and dilute the coconut milk with more water.

INGREDIENTS

1 whole chicken or 1 kg chicken pieces

250 g grated coconut

450 ml water

2 tbsp oil (optional)

2 tsp sugar

2 tsp salt

REMPAH

2 stalks lemon grass *(serai)*

15 shallots *(bawang merah)*

8 red chillies

6 candlenuts *(buah keras)*

1 tsp prawn (shrimp) paste *(belacan)*

$1/2$ tsp pepper

1 tsp coriander *(ketumbar)* powder

PREPARATION

1 Cut the chicken into small pieces then rinse.

2 Prepare the coconut milk. (See page 185).

3 Prepare the *rempah*. Peel then roughly chop the lemon grass (use white portion only) and shallots. Roughly chop the red chillies (deseed, if preferred). Finely pound/blend together with the candlenuts and prawn paste, adding the pepper and coriander powder last.

METHOD

1 Mix all the ingredients together in a pot or wok. Bring to the boil then simmer uncovered until the sauce has thickened (about 30–40 min).

2 Garnish with fried shallots (optional).

Satay Ayam Bakar

Grilled chicken served with a thick spicy coconut gravy

INGREDIENTS

1 whole chicken or 1 kg chicken pieces

250 g grated coconut

8 tbsp water

2 tbsp oil

2 tsp sugar

1 tsp salt

REMPAH

1 stalk lemon grass *(serai)*

2 red chillies

1 slice turmeric *(kunyit)* or $^1/_4$ tsp turmeric powder

8 shallots *(bawang merah)*

2 candlenuts *(buah keras)*

$^1/_2$ tsp prawn (shrimp) paste *(belacan)*

$^1/_2$ tsp pepper

1 tsp coriander *(ketumbar)* powder

PREPARATION

1 Cut the chicken into small pieces then rinse.

2 Prepare the coconut cream. (See page 185).

3 Prepare the *rempah*. Peel then roughly chop the lemon grass (use white portion only), turmeric and shallots. Roughly chop the chillies. Finely pound/blend together with the candlenuts and prawn paste, adding the pepper and coriander powder last.

METHOD

1 Mix all the ingredients together in a large pot, adding the chicken last. Thoroughly coat the chicken with the mixture and leave for at least 30 min.

2 Bring to the boil then simmer over a low flame until the sauce is very thick (about 30–40 min).

3 Remove the chicken pieces and set aside the sauce. Grill the chicken over an open charcoal flame or on the top shelf of the oven at 240°C until the skin is golden brown.

4 Serve the chicken with the sauce on the side or drizzled over the chicken.

Hati Babi

Deep-fried pork liver meatballs served with a sweet sauce

This is one of my favourite dishes. If you prefer using less liver, substitute with more minced pork. It may be difficult to obtain caul lining, but your local butcher will probably give it to you free or at a cheap price since it is usually discarded. It is important that the caul lining is fresh. Check that there is no pungent smell and the colour is white.

INGREDIENTS

300 g pork liver
15 shallots (bawang merah)
4 tsp coriander (ketumbar) powder
1 caul lining (pang sei you)
3 tbsp oil
4 tsp dark soy sauce
1 tsp vinegar
8 tsp sugar
1 tsp salt
1 tsp pepper
300 g minced pork
sweet dark sauce (tim cheong)

PREPARATION

1 Rinse then cut the liver into large pieces. Place in cold water and bring to the boil. Remove then plunge in cold water to stop the cooking process. Finely dice.

2 Peel then pound the shallots.

3 Toast the coriander powder in the toaster oven or by dry-frying over a low flame.

4 Thoroughly rinse the caul lining in cold water several times. Squeeze to drain the excess water.

METHOD

1 Heat a wok over a high flame until it smokes. Add the oil. Lower the flame then stir-fry the shallots until light golden brown. Turn off the flame and add the dark soy sauce, vinegar, sugar, salt, pepper, coriander powder and diced liver. Allow to cool then add the minced pork. Mix well.

2 Shape the mixture into 2.5 cm meatballs (makes about 20 pieces.) Lay them on a tray.

3 Spread the caul lining on a clean chopping board. Place a meatball on the caul lining, then roll it around until it is completely wrapped. Using a sharp knife, cut the wrapped meatball away. Repeat this process with the rest of the meatballs.

4 Steam the wrapped meatballs for 5 min then cool. Over a low flame, deep-fry or grill the steamed meatballs for about 3–5 min.

5 Serve with sweet dark sauce and *Sayur Kuak Chai on the side.

*Sayur Kuak Chai

A pickled vegetable served with Hati Babi, Ayam Siow or roast pork

INGREDIENTS

600 g fresh mustard cabbage (kai choi)
2 tsp salt
1 thumb size knob ginger (halia)
4 tbsp sugar
2 tbsp vinegar
1 tsp mustard powder

PREPARATION

1 Rinse then shred the mustard cabbage (leaves and stalk). Add some salt then rub the mustard cabbage together. Allow to rest (to draw out the water) then squeeze dry.

2 Peel then finely shred the ginger. Add the remaining salt then squeeze dry.

3 Mix the sugar, vinegar and mustard powder into a paste.

METHOD

1 Combine all the ingredients. Serve as a side dish.

Babi Pongteh

Pig's trotters served in a rich brown sauce

Babi Pongteh is a tasty and easy dish to make. It has its origins in Chinese cuisine, with the addition of Peranakan spices. Babi Chin is a similar dish except that it excludes coriander powder. For a healthier version, trim off the excess fat from the trotters or use lean tenderised pork.

INGREDIENTS

1 kg pork trotters

24 shallots *(bawang merah)*

8 cloves garlic *(bawang putih)*

1 1/2 tbsp salted soy beans *(taucheo)*

1 tbsp coriander *(ketumbar)* powder (exclude for Babi Chin)

6 tbsp oil

850 ml water

1 1/2 tbsp sugar

1 1/2 tbsp dark soy sauce

1/2 tsp salt

PREPARATION

1 Chop the pork trotters into 5 cm pieces then rinse.

2 Peel then coarsely pound the shallots and garlic.

3 Lightly pound the salted soy beans.

4 Add some water to the coriander powder and mix into a paste.

METHOD

1 Heat a wok over a high flame until it smokes. Add the oil. Lower the flame, then add the shallots and garlic. Stir-fry until light golden brown. Sprinkle a little water (to prevent the shallots and garlic from burning).

2 Add the coriander paste (exclude for Babi Chin), then the salted soy beans. Stir-fry for 1 min. Sprinkle a little water in again, then stir-fry for another minute.

3 Over a high flame, add the pork and stir-fry for 3 min. Add the sugar and dark soy sauce. Lower the flame and add half of the remaining water then simmer for 2 min.

4 Add the rest of the water then bring to the boil. Simmer until the meat is tender. Add salt to taste.

Babi Asam

Pork in a tangy tamarind sauce

For a healthier version, trim away the excess fat or use lean pork.

INGREDIENTS

600 g belly pork

5 green chillies

3 red chillies

1¹/₂ tbsp salted soy beans (taucheo)

1 rounded tbsp tamarind (asam) pulp

570 ml water

5 tbsp oil

2 tbsp sugar

1 tsp salt

REMPAH

4 candlenuts (buah keras)

20 shallots (bawang merah)

1 tbsp prawn (shrimp) paste (belacan)

PREPARATION

1 Rinse then cut the belly pork into pieces.

2 Slice the red and green chillies lengthwise and deseed, if preferred.

3 Pound the salted soy beans.

4 Prepare the tamarind marinade. (See page 185).

5 Prepare the rempah. Peel and roughly chop shallots. Pound/blend all the rempah ingredients together.

METHOD

1 Heat a wok over a high flame until it smokes. Add the oil. Stir-fry the rempah until light brown and fragrant. Lower to a medium flame and sprinkle in some water.

2 Add the salted soy beans, then the meat. After a few minutes, sprinkle in some water again to prevent the mixture from burning. Add the tamarind marinade then bring to the boil. Cook until the liquid has reduced by half.

3 Add the chillies then simmer until the pork is tender. Add sugar and salt to taste.

Rawan

Beef and *buah keluak* nuts in a rich gravy

This dish originated from Indonesia. It is among my favourites because the beef is tender and *buah keluak* meat is also used. *Buah keluak* meat is now available pre-packed, making this an easy dish to prepare, since you do not need to extract it directly from the nut. If Indonesian sweet dark soy sauce *(kicap manis)* is not available, prepare a substitute by mixing equal amounts of dark soy sauce and sugar.

INGREDIENTS

600 g shin beef

3 rounded tbsp tamarind *(asam)* pulp

1.5 l water

5 tbsp oil

10 *buah keluak* nuts (use meat only)

2 tbsp sugar

2 tbsp Indonesian sweet dark soy sauce *(kicap manis)*

1 tbsp salt

2 kaffir lime leaves *(daun limau purut)*

REMPAH

4 slices galangal *(lengkuas)*

$^1/_2$ thumb size knob turmeric *(kunyit)*

5 cloves garlic *(bawang putih)*

10 shallots *(bawang merah)*

5 red chillies

1 tbsp prawn (shrimp) paste *(belacan)*

1 lemon grass *(serai)*

PREPARATION

1 Cut the beef into small pieces then rinse.

2 Prepare the tamarind marinade. (See page 185).

3 Prepare the *rempah*. Peel then roughly chop the galangal, turmeric, garlic and shallots. Roughly chop the red chillies (deseed, if preferred). Pound/blend together with the prawn paste. Add the peeled and bruised lemon grass (use white portion only) last.

METHOD

1 Heat a wok over a high flame until it smokes. Add the oil. Stir-fry the *rempah* then sprinkle a little water (to prevent it from burning).

2 Add the *buah keluak* meat then stir-fry for 2 min. Add the beef, tamarind marinade, sugar, Indonesian sweet dark soy sauce, salt and kaffir lime leaves. Stir-fry for a few min then simmer until the meat is tender.

satay

Satay Lembu/Kambing

Skewers of beef/mutton served with cucumbers, onions, rice cubes and a spicy peanut sauce

For a luxurious version of this dish, use beef fillet. For a budget-friendly version, use a cheaper cut of meat but tenderise it before marinating. Large batches can be marinated and skewered then frozen for later use.

INGREDIENTS

600 g beef or mutton (middle cut)

2 cucumbers

2 onions or 10 shallots
(bawang merah)

2 rounded tbsp tamarind (asam)
pulp

120 ml water

40 satay sticks

REMPAH

1 stalk lemon grass (serai)

4 slices galangal (lengkuas)

4 slices ginger (halia)

2 candlenuts (buah keras)

6 shallots (bawang merah)

2 cloves garlic (bawang putih)

2 tsp coriander (ketumbar) powder

1 tsp cumin (jintan putih) powder

1 tsp turmeric (kunyit) powder

2 tbsp sugar

1 tsp salt

2 tbs peanuts, roasted and ground

2 tbsp oil

PREPARATION

1 Tenderize the meat by pounding slightly, if necessary. Cut into small cubes.

2 Rinse then slice the cucumber into bite-sized chunks.

3 Peel then cut the onion or shallots into cubes.

4 Prepare the tamarind marinate. (See page 185).

5 Prepare the rempah. Peel then roughly chop the lemon grass (use white portion only), galangal, ginger, candlenuts, shallots and garlic. Finely pound/blend all the rempah ingredients together.

METHOD

1 In a large bowl, knead the tamarind marinade and the meat together. Add the rempah and knead again until it is mixed well. Marinate for at least 30 min.

2 Thread the meat using the satay sticks.

3 Grill over an open charcoal flame or on the top shelf of the oven at 240°C for 5–7 min on each side. Baste with oil each time.

4 To serve, arrange the satay on a large serving plate with the cucumbers, onions and Nasi Tindeh (see page 166) or Ketupat on the side. Serve with *Peanut Satay Sauce in individual soup bowls or in a large serving bowl.

*Peanut Satay Sauce

A spicy peanut dipping sauce for beef, mutton and chicken satay

Although ready-made satay sauces are available, there is something satisfying about making your own.

INGREDIENTS

2 stalks lemon grass (serai)

180 ml oil

4 rounded tbsp tamarind (asam)
pulp

water

4 tbsp sugar or to taste

1 tbsp salt

600 g peanuts, roasted and
ground

REMPAH

12 slices galangal (lengkuas)

12 shallots (bawang merah)

6 cloves garlic (bawang putih)

20–30 dried chillies

1 tbsp prawn (shrimp) paste
(belacan)

PREPARATION

1 Soak the dried chillies for the rempah in hot water.

2 Peel then bruise the lemon grass (use white portion only).

3 Prepare the tamarind marinade with 280 ml water. (See page 185).

4 Prepare the rempah. Deseed then roughly chop the soaked dried chillies. Peel then roughly chop the galangal, shallots and garlic. Finely pound/blend together with the prawn paste.

METHOD

1 Heat a wok over a high flame until it smokes. Add the oil. Stir-fry the rempah and lemon grass until fragrant.

2 Add the tamarind marinade then bring to the boil. Boil for 2 min before adding the sugar, salt, ground peanuts and 850 ml water. Simmer until the sauce thickens.

Satay Ayam/Babi

Skewers of chicken/pork served with cucumbers, onions, rice cubes and a spicy peanut sauce

Serve satay with Mee Rebus, Lontong or a variety of *lauk piring*. For a healthier version of satay, use skinned chicken and lean pork. Tenderise the meat before marinating.

INGREDIENTS

600 g chicken or pork

REMPAH

1 stalk lemon grass (*serai*)

10 shallots (*bawang merah*)

2 tsp coriander (*ketumbar*) powder

1 tsp cumin (*jintan putih*) powder

1 tsp turmeric (*kunyit*) powder

$1/4$ tsp cinnamon or cassia (*kayu manis*) powder

1 tsp salt

2 tsp sugar

2 tbsp peanuts, roasted and ground

1 tbsp oil

2 cucumbers

2 onions or 10 shallots (*bawang merah*)

40 satay sticks

PREPARATION

1 Cut the meat into small cubes and tenderize by pounding lightly.

2 Prepare the *rempah*. Peel then roughly chop the lemon grass (use white portion only) and shallots. Finely pound/blend all the *rempah* ingredients together.

3 Rinse then slice the cucumbers into bite-sized chunks. Peel then cut the onions or shallots into cubes.

METHOD

1 Mix the meat and *rempah* in a large bowl. Marinate for at least 30 min.

2 Thread the meat using the satay sticks.

3 Grill the satay over an open charcoal flame or on the top shelf of the oven at 240°C for 5–7 min on each side. Baste with oil on each side.

4 To serve, arrange the satay on a large plate with the cut cucumbers, onions and Nasi Tindeh (see page 166) or Ketupat.

5 Serve Satay Ayam with Peanut Satay Sauce (see page 98) and Satay Babi with *Pineapple Satay Sauce.

*Pineapple Satay Sauce

A tangy pineapple dipping sauce for pork satay

INGREDIENTS

$1/2$ pineapple

1 red chilli

$1/2$ tbsp sugar

1 tsp kalamansi lime (*limau kesturi*) or lemon juice

$1/4$ tsp salt

PREPARATION

1 Peel and grate the pineapple.

2 Pound the chilli.

METHOD

1 Mix all the ingredients together and let it rest for 15 min in the refrigerator.

2 Serve in individual bowls or a large serving bowl.

Satay Babi Bakar

Grilled skewers of pork marinated in a tangy sweet sauce with a cucumber salad

INGREDIENTS

1 kg pork or belly pork

REMPAH

12 slices galangal *(lengkuas)*

3 stalks lemon grass *(serai)*

2 tbsp coriander *(ketumbar)* powder

$^1/_2$ tsp cumin *(jintan putih)* powder

$3^1/_2$ tbsp palm sugar *(gula Melaka)*

$^1/_2$ tsp sugar

1 tsp salt

$3^1/_2$ tbsp Indonesian sweet dark soy sauce *(kicap manis)*

3 tbsp kalamansi lime *(limau kesturi)* or lemon juice

2 tbsp dark soy sauce

30 satay sticks

PREPARATION

1 Prepare the *rempah*. Peel and roughly chop the galangal and lemon grass (use white portion only). Finely pound/blend together, then add the remaining ingredients.

2 Slice the pork then rinse. Add the *rempah* and knead thoroughly. Allow to marinate for at least 30 min.

3 Thread the meat using the satay sticks.

METHOD

1 Grill the satay over an open charcoal flame or on the top shelf of the oven at 240°C for 5–7 min on each side. Baste each side with oil.

2 Serve with the *cucumber side dish.

*Cucumber Side Dish

INGREDIENTS

1 cucumber

10 bird's eye chillies *(cili padi)* or 5 red chillies

2 tsp kalamansi lime *(limau kesturi)* or lemon juice

2 tbsp dark soy sauce

2 tsp sugar

PREPARATION

1 Rinse then slice the cucumber.

2 Pound the chillies (deseed, if preferred).

METHOD

1 In a serving bowl, mix the ingredients together. Serve.

Satay Babi Cho Cho

Grilled skewers of pork marinated in a spicy sauce

The wonderful thing about Satay is that the meat can be prepared in large batches, marinated, skewered then refrigerated or frozen until it is ready for use—perfect for parties and barbecues.

INGREDIENTS

480 g pork or belly pork
250 g grated coconut
120 ml water
1 tbsp oil

REMPAH

1 stalk lemon grass (serai)
4 candlenuts (buah keras)
8 shallots (bawang merah)
4 red chillies
$^1/_2$ tsp prawn (shrimp) paste (belacan)
1 tsp coriander (ketumbar) powder
2 tsp sugar
1 tsp salt

40 satay sticks

PREPARATION

1 Cut the pork into small pieces then rinse.

2 Prepare the coconut cream. (See page 185).

3 Prepare the rempah. Peel then roughly chop the lemon grass (use white portion only) and shallots. Roughly chop the red chillies. Pound/blend together with the prawn paste, adding the coriander powder, sugar and salt last.

METHOD

1 Combine all the ingredients and allow the meat to marinate for at least 30 min.

2 Thread the meat using the satay sticks.

3 Grill over an open charcoal flame or on the top shelf of the oven at 240°C for 5–7 min on each side. Baste with oil each time.

one-dish meals

Mee Siam

Fried rice noodles served with a spicy coconut gravy

Mee Siam is a popular dish in Singapore and also a favourite of my family's. It originates from Thailand, formerly known as Siam. It is perfect for Sunday lunches or small parties. We usually serve it with prawn crackers *(keropok)* on the side.

INGREDIENTS

600 g rice vermicelli *(beehoon)*

600 g medium-sized prawns (shrimps)

8 eggs

150 g chives *(ku chai)*

400 g (2 pieces) firm tofu *(taukua)*

10 kalamansi limes *(limau kesturi)*

160 g dried prawns (shrimps) *(udang kering)*

600 g bean sprouts

300 ml oil

570 ml water

REMPAH

300 g shallots *(bawang merah)*

3 tbsp prawn (shrimp) paste *(belacan)*

15 red chillies or 60 dried chillies

3 tbsp oil

GRAVY

300 g salted soy beans *(taucheo)*

1 medium-sized onion

150 g grated coconut

800 ml water

4 tbsp sugar

PREPARATION

1. If dried chillies are used for the *rempah*, soak them in hot water.

2. Soak the rice vermicelli for 5 min, then drain.

3. Add the prawns to boiling water then simmer for 10 min. Set aside to cool. Shell, devein then halve the prawns lengthwise. (Freeze the shells for use in other recipes).

4. Hardboil the eggs. Remove and allow to cool. Shell then slice into wedges. Cut the chives into 2 cm lengths. (Discard the light green and white portion, which is about 5 cm from the base).

5. Cut the firm tofu into 2.5 cm strips and halve the limes.

6. Finely mince the dried prawns.

7. Rinse the bean sprouts. Remove the caps and roots, if necessary.

8. Prepare the *rempah*. Deseed then roughly chop the soaked/fresh chillies. Peel and roughly chop the shallots. Pound/blend together with the prawn paste and oil. It should have a creamy orange texture.

9. Lightly pound the salted soy beans. Peel and slice the onion.

10. Prepare the coconut milk. (See page 185).

METHOD

1. In a pot, add the salted soy beans, coconut milk, onions and sugar. Place it over the stove, but leave the flame off.

2. Heat a wok over a high flame until it smokes. Add the oil. Add the tofu then lower the flame. Stir-fry until light golden brown but still soft in the centre. (Avoid overcooking as it will become rubbery). Remove and drain.

3. Leave 100 ml oil in the wok then stir-fry the *rempah* and dried prawns. After 15 min, remove 4 tbsp of the mixture and set it aside in a small serving dish. (Serve it on the side for those who want their Mee Siam more spicy).

4. Stir-fry the mixture for about 30 min or more, until it turns into a deep golden brown and the oil has separated.

5. Scoop out 5 tbsp of the *rempah* and place it in the pot to make the gravy. Over a medium flame, allow the gravy to simmer for about 30 min. Once it has thickened slightly, keep it warm over a very low flame.

6. Add 570 ml water to the remaining *rempah* in the wok. Stir thoroughly, then bring to the boil. Add the bean sprouts and cook for a further 2–3 min.

7. Add the rice vermicelli then lower the flame. Using cooking chopsticks (to prevent the vermicelli from breaking), turn the rice vermicelli and bean sprouts over in the wok. This helps the rice vermicelli to cook evenly and mixes all the ingredients.

8. Dish the rice vermicelli out onto a large serving plate or onto individual plates. Garnish with the fried tofu, chives and prawns. Arrange the sliced eggs and lime around the edge of the dish.

9. Serve the gravy in a separate bowl. Pour the gravy over the rice vermicelli just before eating.

Popiah

Egg skins filled with stewed vegetables, meat and a wide variety of garnishes

I have had many Popiah meals and each cook prepares it in his/her own style. A few of my aunts have become well-known for their Popiah and my cousin makes a vegetarian version which suits the health-conscious. It is an extremely laborious dish to make, since each garnish has to be fresh and prepared separately. But it is great for parties since it involves an interactive process of making each Popiah. Excess filling can be used for Kueh Pietee.

INGREDIENTS

FILLING

900 g cooked bamboo shoots (rebung)

600 g turnip (bang kuang)

800 g (4 pieces) firm tofu (taukua)

600 ml water

600 g belly pork

600 g small prawns (shrimps)

10 cloves garlic (bawang putih)

6 tbsp salted soy beans (taucheo)

2 tbsp dark soy sauce

1 tbsp sugar

1 tsp salt

6 tbsp oil

GARNISHES

2 heads local lettuce

200 g coriander (Chinese parsley)

1 cucumber

10 red chillies

20 cloves garlic (bawang putih)

600 g medium-sized prawns (shrimps)

200 g bean sprouts

2 Chinese pork sausages (lap cheong)

6 eggs

200 g crabmeat (from 1.2 kg crabs)

1 bottle thick sweet sauce (tim cheong)

> **Tips:**
> - For a healthier option, substitute the belly pork with skinned/lean boneless chicken.
> - Place an inverted rice bowl in a large serving bowl. This will help drain the excess liquid in the filling.

PREPARATION

Garnishes

1 Pluck, rinse and dry the lettuce leaves. Rinse and dry the coriander, plucking only the leafy parts. Peel, slice and deseed the cucumber. Finely shred into 5 cm long strips.

2 Finely pound/blend the red chillies (deseed, if preferred).

3 Peel and finely mince all the garlic and set aside one-third for the garnish, leaving the rest for frying.

4 Place each garnish on a separate serving plate or bowl.

Filling

1 Cut the bamboo shoots and turnip into thin 5 cm long strips. Slice the firm tofu into 2.5 cm long strips.

2 Place the belly pork in 600 ml cold water and bring to the boil. Allow to simmer for a few minutes before removing belly pork. Skim off the impurities from the water with a spoon. Once the belly pork has cooled, cut into 2.5 cm long strips.

3 Using the same water, boil the medium-sized prawns for the garnish. Shell, devein then slice in half lengthwise. Place on a serving plate. (Reserve the shells for the stock).

4 Pound the prawn shells then add the pork stock. Strain using a sieve. Discard the shells and set aside the stock.

5 Steam the bean sprouts then the Chinese sausages in the top tier of a steamer. When the bean sprouts are cooked, remove then blanch in cold water and drain. Cut the steamed Chinese sausages into thin slices or strips. Use the same water to hardboil the eggs. Shell the eggs and cut into wedges. (Alternatively, make thin omelettes with the eggs and slice into fine strips by rolling up and slicing). Place each filling ingredient on a separate serving plate or bowl.

6 Using the same steamer (adding more water if necessary), steam the crabs and remove the flesh once cool. To remove the flesh from the crab legs, chop off the legs and the tips of the legs. Roll the handle of a chopper across the length of each crab leg. The flesh should squeeze out easily.

METHOD

Filling

1 Heat a wok over a high flame until it smokes. Add the oil. Lower the flame, then stir-fry the garlic until light golden brown. Remove and drain half for the garnish.

2 Add the salted soy beans to the remaining fried garlic in the wok and sprinkle some water to prevent it from burning. Over a high flame, add the small prawns and then the shredded pork. Stir-fry for a few minutes.

3 Add the bamboo shoots, turnip, dark soy sauce, sugar and salt. Fry thoroughly before adding the firm tofu strips. Add the stock. Bring to the boil then simmer for about 20 min until the vegetables are tender and the gravy has reduced. Place into a large serving bowl.

Popiah Egg Skins

INGREDIENTS

10 eggs

$^1/_2$ tsp salt

300 g plain flour

4 tsp oil

700 ml water

screwpine *(pandan)* leaves

Tips:

- The objective is to get the skins as thin and even as possible.

- The screwpine leaves add a subtle flavour and colour to the egg skins, while making it easy to count the number of egg skins that have been made. I learnt this from my Aunt Monica Lee.

- In humid weather, flour will get damp *(basi)* if not stored in an airtight container. To dry the flour, put it in the sun or oven at a low temperature.

- For a healthier option for the egg skins, substitute egg white for egg yolk proportionately.

PREPARATION

1 In a large bowl, crack the eggs then beat well together. (Stir rather than whisk to avoid trapping air bubbles).

2 Add the salt to the flour then sift twice (to aerate it and remove impurities).

3 Gradually add the flour to the eggs, stirring well each time. Finally, add the oil and water. (This method will avoid lumps forming in the batter).

4 Sieve the batter to remove any lumps and impurities. Set the mixture aside to rest.

METHOD

1 Lightly grease a large crepe pan or any large flat pan with oil. Heat over a low flame. Remove the pan from the heat, then pour a spoonful of batter onto it. Lift and tilt the pan to spread the batter around evenly.

2 Heat the pan over a low flame and cook for 3 min. The egg skin is cooked when the edges peel away from the side and the colour is noticeably different.

3 Using your fingers, start by carefully peeling away the edges, then lift the egg skin onto a serving plate. Do not flip the egg skin.

4 Place two screwpine leaves crosswise on the egg skin before placing each new egg skin.

5 Continue to make the egg skins, stirring the batter each time as the flour tends to sink to the bottom. Cover the egg skins with cling film or a damp piece of cloth to prevent them from drying out.

Popiah

Allow the guests to wrap their own Popiah. Arrange the individual dishes in the order that the ingredients are used. There are various ways to wrap Popiah, but I suggest the following method:

- Start with a Popiah Egg Skin (see page 112), then 1–2 pieces of lettuce (to prevent the filling from soaking into and breaking the egg skin), followed by a combination of any of the following ingredients: pounded chilli, raw minced garlic, fried minced garlic and thick sweet soy sauce (this should be drizzled then spread across the lettuce with the back of a spoon), followed by the filling. Garnish with the crabmeat, Chinese sausage, prawns, eggs, shredded cucumber, bean sprouts and coriander.

- Fold the bottom end of the Popiah Egg Skin over the filling, then fold the two sides over. Roll it away from you until the filling is completely wrapped, like a spring roll. Using a sharp knife, cut it into 2–3 cm thick slices.

Laksa

Rice vermicelli served with prawns and fish balls in a spicy coconut gravy

INGREDIENTS

1.5 kg grated coconut

1.7 l water

600 g bean sprouts

150 g dried prawns (shrimps) (udang kering)

1 cucumber

20 stalks laksa leaves (daun kesum)

400 g fresh uncooked fish balls

600 g medium-sized prawns

2 tbsp sugar

1¹/₂ tbsp salt

1.7 l water

900 g fresh thick rice vermicelli (laksa beehoon)

CHILLI OIL

20 dried chillies

300 ml oil

REMPAH

2 stalks lemon grass (serai)

40 slices galangal (lengkuas)

12 candlenuts (buah keras)

15 dried chillies

25 shallots (bawang merah)

2 tbsp prawn (shrimp) paste (belacan)

2 thumb size knob turmeric (kunyit) or 1 tbsp turmeric power

2 tbsp coriander (ketumbar) powder

PREPARATION

1 Soak the dried chillies for the *rempah* in hot water.

2 Prepare the coconut cream and milk to obtain 300 ml coconut cream and 1.4 l coconut milk. (See page 185).

3 Blanch the bean sprouts. Drain and set aside.

4 Pound/blend the dried prawns.

5 Peel then cut the cucumber in half lengthwise. Using a spoon, scrap away and discard the seeds. Finely shred the cucumber.

6 Wash then finely shred the laksa leaves.

7 Prepare the *rempah*. Deseed then roughly chop the soaked dried chillies. Peel then roughly chop the lemon grass (use white portion only), galangal, shallots and turmeric (if fresh turmeric is used). Pound/blend together with the prawn paste, adding the turmeric powder (if used) and coriander powder last.

METHOD

1 Prepare the stock. Bring the water to the boil and cook the fish balls. The fish balls are cooked once they rise to the surface. Remove and set aside.

2 Using the same water, cook the prawns for 5–7 min. Remove, shell then devein the prawns. Set aside.

3 Prepare the chilli oil. Heat a wok over a high flame until it smokes. Add the oil. Lower the flame, then stir-fry the chillies. Remove the wok from the stove and let it rest. Once the chillies have settled at the bottom, remove the chillies from the oil and place it in a small serving dish.

4 Reheat the chilli oil, then add the *rempah*. Stir-fry for about 10 min until it is fragrant. Sprinkle some water into the *rempah*, then lower the flame.

5 Add the dried prawns then stir-fry for 2 min. Increase to a high flame then add the coconut milk and stock. Bring to the boil, stirring constantly.

6 Add the coconut cream, sugar and salt. Lower the flame then simmer for 10 min.

7 Blanch the rice vermicelli in boiling water then drain well.

8 To serve, place some rice vermicelli, cucumber, bean sprouts, *fish balls, prawns and laksa leaves into individual serving bowls. Pour the gravy over and serve hot. Serve the fried chilli on the side.

*Fish Balls

INGREDIENTS

600 g finely minced fish

420 ml water

1 tbsp salt

pepper to taste

Tip: Use white fish meat, such as Spanish mackerel *(ikan tenggiri)*, wolf herring *(ikan parang)*, whiting, haddock and pike. If minced fish meat is not available, use skinned fish fillets then finely mince the meat in a blender or use a Chinese cleaver. If the meat has fine bones and veins, press it through a sieve using the back of a spoon or pastry scrapper.

PREPARATION

1 Place the fish meat in a bowl and gradually add the water while beating. Add salt and pepper to taste.

2 Form the fish balls by scooping the minced fish mixture with one hand and squeezing it between your index finger and thumb. With a spoon in the other hand, scoop the mixture into a ball then drop it into a basin of salted water. Repeat this process until the mixture is used up. Leave the fish balls aside for 1 hr to set, then drain. Discard the water.

METHOD

1 Drop the fish balls into the boiling water and remove them once they rise to the surface.

Penang Laksa

Rice vermicelli served Penang-style with a wide variety of garnishes in a spicy gravy

INGREDIENTS

900 g fish, preferably wolf
    herring *(ikan parang)*
4 rounded tbsp tamarind *(asam)*
    pulp
850 ml water
5 tbsp sugar
¹/₂ tbsp salt
600 g fresh thick rice vermicelli
    (laksa *beehoon)*

STOCK

850 ml water
8 fresh tamarind *(asam)* pods
1 tsp salt

GARNISHES

1 cucumber
1 fresh pineapple
1 head local lettuce
10 preserved Chinese shallots
    (lohquo)
5–10 red chillies
mint leaves
laksa leaves *(daun kesum)*
2 pink ginger buds *(bunga
    siantan)*
1 tbsp thick black prawn
    (shrimp) paste *(heiko)*
2 tbsp water

REMPAH

2 stalks lemon grass *(serai)*
15 slices galangal *(lengkuas)*
1 thumb size knob turmeric
    (kunyit) or ³/₄ tbsp turmeric
    powder
20 shallots *(bawang merah)*
15 red chillies
1 tbsp prawn (shrimp) paste
    (belacan)

PREPARATION

1 Prepare the tamarind marinade. (See page 185).

2 Peel, deseed and finely shred the cucumber. Shred the pineapple and local lettuce. Slice the preserved Chinese shallots and chillies. Finely slice the mint leaves, laska leaves and pink ginger buds. Place on a serving plate.

3 Add water to the thick black prawn paste to make a smooth sauce. Place in a serving bowl.

4 Prepare the *rempah*. Peel and roughly chop the lemon grass (use white portion only), galangal, fresh turmeric and shallots. Pound/blend together with the chillies (deseed, if preferred) and prawn paste.

5 Remove the hard outer shell of the fresh tamarind pod.

METHOD

1 Bring the water to the boil, then cook the fish for 5–10 min. Remove the fish and allow to cool. Using a fork or chopsticks, flake off the meat. Return the bones to the stock.

2 Bring the stock to the boil, then simmer for 10 min. Strain and discard the bones.

3 Add the tamarind marinade, sugar, salt and *rempah* to the stock. Bring to the boil, then add the flakes of fish.

4 Blanch the rice vermicelli in boiling water then drain well.

5 To serve, place some rice vermicelli and the various garnishes into individual serving bowls. Pour the soup over and serve hot.

Mee Rebus

Egg noodles with a thick spicy sauce

This version is quite different from the types available in hawker centres in Singapore because of the amount of beef used. Satay (see pages 98–104) goes well with this dish.

INGREDIENTS

600 g beef

900 g bean sprouts

1.2 kg yellow noodles (Hokkien mee)

GARNISHES

8 eggs

10 kalamansi limes (limau kesturi)

5 spring onions (scallions)

5 sprigs Chinese celery

10 green chillies

30 shallots (bawang merah)

1.2 kg (6 pieces) firm tofu (taukua)

GRAVY

300 g potatoes

1.5 l water

4 tbsp curry powder

120 ml water

4 tbsp salted soy beans (taucheo)

4 tbsp dried prawns (shrimps) (udang kering)

160 g peanuts, toasted and ground

1 tsp salt

2 tbsp sugar

250 ml oil

REMPAH

12 slices galangal (lengkuas)

5 slices ginger (halia)

20 shallots (bawang merah)

5 cloves garlic (bawang putih)

10 dried chillies

8 candlenuts (buah keras)

1 tbsp prawn (shrimp) paste (belacan)

PREPARATION

1 Soak the dried chillies for the *rempah* in hot water.

2 Slice the beef.

3 Blanch the bean sprouts in boiling water. Drain.

4 Hardboil the eggs. Allow to cool, shell then slice.

5 Boil the potatoes. Peel then mash the potatoes with 1.5 l water.

6 Halve the limes. Finely slice the spring onions and Chinese celery. Slice the chillies diagonally.

7 Peel and finely slice the shallots for the garnish.

8 Mix the curry powder and 120 ml water to form a paste.

9 Pound the salted soy beans slightly.

10 Pound/blend the dried prawns.

11 Prepare the *rempah*. Deseed then roughly chop the soaked dried chillies. Peel then roughly chop the galangal, ginger, shallots and garlic. Pound/blend together with the candlenuts and prawn paste.

METHOD

1 Heat a wok over a high flame until it smokes. Add the oil. Lower the flame then stir-fry the finely sliced shallots for the garnish until golden brown. Drain and set aside.

2 Stir-fry the tofu until light golden brown. Remove and dice. Set aside for the garnish.

3 Add some more oil, then stir-fry the *rempah* until fragrant. Add the curry paste then the salted soy beans. Sprinkle with some water (to prevent it from burning).

4 Add the dried prawns and sliced beef and stir-fry. Add the potatoes, peanuts, sugar and salt. Bring to the boil then simmer for about 15 min.

5 Blanch the yellow noodles in boiling water then drain well.

6 To serve, place the noodles and bean sprouts in individual serving dishes. Pour the gravy over the noodles. Garnish with eggs, tofu, shallots, spring onions, Chinese celery, green chillies and lime.

Soto

A chicken and beef soup served with cubes of rice and a beef and potato cutlet

Cubes of boiled potatoes may also be added to make this dish more substantial.

INGREDIENTS

1 whole chicken or 1 kg chicken pieces

3 l water

500 g beef

10 shallots *(bawang merah)*

10 cloves garlic *(bawang putih)*

500 ml oil

2 thumb size knobs galangal *(lengkuas)*

2 star anise *(pekek/bunga lawang)*

10 cloves *(bunga cengkih)*

$^1/_2$ tsp grated nutmeg *(buah pala)*

$^1/_2$ tbsp peppercorn

1 tbsp sugar

$1^1/_2$ tbsp salt

BEEF AND POTATO CUTLET

200 g minced beef

500 g potatoes

2 eggs

$^1/_2$ tsp sugar

1 tsp salt

A dash of pepper

A pinch of grated nutmeg *(buah pala)*

GARNISHES

20 shallots *(bawang merah)*

5 spring onions (scallions)

2 sprigs Chinese celery

600 g bean sprouts

PREPARATION

1 Peel then finely slice all the shallots.

2 Peel then mince the garlic. Peel then crush the galangal.

3 Slice the spring onions and Chinese celery. Set aside for the garnish.

4 Blanch the bean sprouts and boil the potatoes. Peel then mash the potatoes.

METHOD

1 Heat a wok over a high flame until it smokes. Add the oil. Lower the flame, then stir-fry the garlic. Remove and drain. Set aside one-third of the fried garlic for the cutlets and the remainder for the stock.

2 Stir-fry the shallots in the same oil, adding more oil if necessary. Remove and drain. Set aside one-third of the fried shallots for the cutlets, one-third for the stock and one-third for the garnish.

3 Bring 1 l water and 500 g of beef to the boil. Skim off the impurities that surface. Simmer for about 30–40 min, then remove the beef and slice.

4 Add the remaining water to the stock and bring to the boil. Add the chicken, then simmer over a medium flame for about 20 min. Turn the chicken over and simmer for another 20 min. Remove then plunge the chicken in cold water.

5 Using your fingers, shred the meat off the bone. Place the bones back into the stock, then add the spices, fried shallots and garlic. Simmer for 30 min then strain.

6 Combine all the ingredients for the cutlet, including one-third of the fried shallots and garlic. Form into patties then fry. (Optional: Dip in beaten egg before frying).

7 To serve, place the bean sprouts, beef, chicken and cutlets in individual serving bowls, then pour the hot soup over. Garnish with fried shallots, spring onions and Chinese celery.

Java Soto

A beef soup seasoned with herbs and spices

Cubes of boiled potatoes may also be added to make this dish more substantial.

INGREDIENTS

STOCK

1 thumb size knob galangal (lengkuas)

2 stalks lemon grass (serai)

1.25 kg beef shin

4.5 l water

6 salam leaves (daun salam)

3 kaffir lime leaves (daun limau purut)

3 sticks celery

3 leeks

2¹/₂ tbsp oil

3 tbsp salt

1¹/₂ tbsp Indonesian sweet dark soy sauce (kicap manis)

REMPAH

2 thumb size knobs ginger (halia)

10 shallots (bawang merah)

6 cloves garlic (bawang putih)

1 tbsp coriander (ketumbar) powder

2 tsp pepper

CHILLI SAUCE

10–20 bird's eye chillies (cili padi)

¹/₂ tsp sugar

1 tsp vinegar

1 tbsp light soy sauce

GARNISHES

600 g bean sprouts

4 sprigs coriander (Chinese parsley)

40 shallots (bawang merah)

PREPARATION

1 Peel and bruise the galangal and lemon grass (use white portion only) for the stock.

2 To prepare the *rempah*, peel and roughly chop the ginger, shallots and garlic. Coarsely pound/blend together, adding the coriander powder and pepper last.

3 Prepare the chilli sauce. Pound the chillies (deseed, if preferred) then add the sugar, vinegar and light soy sauce. Place in a small serving dish.

4 Prepare the garnish. Blanch the bean sprouts (remove the caps and roots, optional) and finely slice the coriander. Peel the shallots and finely slice.

METHOD

1 Prepare the stock. In a large pot, place beef in cold water then bring to the boil. Skim off the impurities that surface. Add all the ingredients for the stock. Simmer for 30–40 min.

2 Heat a wok over a high flame until it smokes. Add the oil. Lower the flame then stir-fry the finely sliced shallots for the garnish until golden brown. Remove and drain.

3 Over a high flame, stir-fry the *rempah* then add it to the stock. Stir in the salt and Indonesian sweet dark soy sauce. Simmer until the meat is tender then remove the meat and slice. Strain the stock.

4 To serve, arrange some the sliced meat and beans sprouts in individual serving bowls. Fill with soup, then garnish with fried shallots and coriander. Serve the chilli sauce on the side.

multiple-dish meals

Nasi Lemak

Nasi Lemak is coconut-flavoured rice served with a variety of dishes: Udang Asam Goreng, Sambal Udang, Ikan Asam Pekat, Sayur Kangkung, Otak-otak, Otak-otak Putih, Sambal Timun, Ikan Bilis and Achar.

Nasi Lemak

Coconut-flavoured rice prepared by steaming

One of my favourite Singaporean dishes is Nasi Lemak. It usually comes in a neatly bound banana leaf package filled with coconut-flavoured rice, small fried fish *(ikan kuning)*, scrambled eggs, cucumber, fried whitebait *(ikan bilis)* and a sweet *sambal*. It is sold as breakfast and is inexpensive.

Peranakan Nasi Lemak raises the concept of the dish to an entirely different realm. The coconut-flavoured rice is served as part of an elaborate meal for lunch or dinner with many side dishes. The ingredients are more expensive and each dish is painstakingly prepared. My grandmother's cookbook mentions that according to Peranakan tradition, a bridegroom's mother would present this rice to the bride's mother 12 days after the wedding to acknowledge that the bride was chaste.

INGREDIENTS

2 screwpine *(pandan)* leaves

900 g rice, preferably Thai long grain rice

1 kg grated coconut

570 ml water

2 tsp salt

> **Tip:**
>
> For a healthier version, dilute the coconut milk by using the same amount of water but less grated coconut.

PREPARATION

1 Rinse then tie each of the screwpine leaves into a knot.

2 Rinse the rice then soak in water for at least 12 hours.

3 Prepare the coconut milk. (See page 185).

METHOD

1 Place the soaked rice in the top tier of a steamer. Create steam holes in the rice with a chopstick by poking the tip of the chopstick all the way down to the bottom of the rice. (These steam holes will enable the rice to cook evenly).

2 Steam the rice for 30 min. Stir the rice and create new steam holes every 10 min.

3 Place the coconut milk and salt in a large pot. Scoop the steamed rice into the pot, stir thoroughly then cover. Set aside until the rice has absorbed the coconut milk (about 20 min).

4 Place the rice back into the steamer with the screwpine leaves. Steam for 20–30 min or until the rice is cooked. Reduce the flame from high to medium then low after every 10 minutes. Stir the rice, then create new steam holes each time the flame is lowered.

5 Remove the screwpine leaves before serving.

Nasi Lemak (Simplified)

Coconut-flavoured rice prepared by a simplified boiling method

INGREDIENTS

2 screwpine *(pandan)* leaves

2.3 l water

600 g rice, preferably Thai long grain rice

500 g grated coconut

220 ml water

1 tsp salt

PREPARATION

1 Rinse the rice.

2 Tie each screwpine leaf into a knot.

3 Prepare the coconut milk. (See page 185).

METHOD

1 Bring the water to the boil. Add the rice, then boil for 5 min. Drain the rice and immediately stir in the coconut cream and salt. Cover and set aside for 10 min to allow the rice to absorb the coconut cream.

2 Place the rice in the upper tier of a steamer. Cover and steam with the knotted screwpine leaves for 5–10 min. Remove the screwpine leaves before serving.

Udang Asam Goreng

Crispy fried prawns marinated in a tangy tamarind sauce

This is an extremely easy dish to prepare. The trick to cooking prawns that are crisp and have a slightly smoky flavour is to ensure that the wok and oil are extremely hot before adding the prawns. By adding the reserved marinade at the end, the prawns will be crisp but slightly glazed with the tamarind sauce.

INGREDIENTS

600 g tiger or king-sized prawns
   (shrimps)

3 tbsp oil

1 rounded tbsp tamarind *(asam)*
   pulp

570 ml water

1 tbsp salt

GARNISH

1 sprig coriander (Chinese
   parsley)

PREPARATION

1 Using sharp scissors, trim off the sharp ends of the feelers and the legs of the prawns. Rinse.

2 Prepare the tamarind marinade. (See page 185). Add the salt.

3 Soak the cleaned prawns in the marinade for at least 15 min. Drain, then reserve 3 tbsp of the marinade. Discard the rest.

METHOD

1 Heat a wok over a high flame until it smokes. Add the oil. When the oil is smoking hot, add the prawns and stir-fry until the meat is cooked and the shells are crisp.

2 Add the reserved marinade and allow the sauce to reduce slightly. Garnish with coriander. Serve.

Sambal Udang

Prawns stir-fried in a thick and spicy *sambal* sauce

INGREDIENTS

800 g prawns (shrimps)

150 ml oil

2 tbsp sugar

1 tsp salt

1 cucumber

1 rounded tbsp tamarind *(asam)* pulp

120 ml water

REMPAH

20 dried chillies

6 candlenuts *(buah keras)*

30 shallots *(bawang merah)*

2 tsp prawn (shrimp) paste *(belacan)*

PREPARATION

1 Soak the dried chillies for the *rempah* in hot water.

2 Shell and devein the prawns. (Freeze the prawn shells for use in other recipes).

3 Peel then slice the cucumber.

4 Prepare the tamarind marinade. (See page 185).

5 Prepare the *rempah*. Deseed then roughly chop the soaked dried chillies. Peel and roughly chop the shallots. Finely pound/blend together with the candlenuts and prawn paste.

METHOD

1 Heat a wok over a high flame until it smokes. Add the oil. Add the *rempah* and fry for 1 min before lowering to a medium flame. Simmer for 2 min, then raise to a high flame.

2 Add the prawns and stir-fry for 1min then add the tamarind marinade. Reduce to a medium flame, then simmer until the prawns are cooked.

3 Add sugar and salt to taste. Garnish with the sliced cucumbers.

Ikan Asam Pekat

Braised fish in a tamarind and turmeric gravy

INGREDIENTS

4 red chillies

4 green chillies

1 stalk lemon grass *(serai)*

600 g fish, preferably Spanish mackerel *(ikan tenggiri)*

5 tbsp sugar

1 tbsp salt

1 tbsp oil (optional)

6 rounded tbsp tamarind *(asam)* pulp

800 ml water

REMPAH

4 shallots *(bawang merah)*

1 thumb size knob turmeric *(kunyit)*

1¹/₂ tbsp prawn (shrimp) paste *(belacan)*

> **Tip:**
> Add the chillies and fish only when the gravy has reduced sufficiently to avoid overcooking the fish.

PREPARATION

1 Slit the chillies lengthwise and deseed, if preferred.

2 Peel then bruise the lemon grass (use white portion only).

3 Prepare the tamarind marinade. (See page 185).

4 Prepare the *rempah*. Peel and roughly chop the shallots and turmeric. Finely pound/blend together with the shrimp paste.

METHOD

1 In a large pot, mix the tamarind marinade and *rempah*. Add the lemon grass, sugar and salt. Bring to the boil, then simmer for about 15 min until the gravy has thickened.

2 Add the chillies and the fish. Simmer for 5 min. Add the oil (optional).

Sayur Kangkung

Fried water convolvulus with *sambal*

INGREDIENTS

1 kg water convolvulus
   (kangkung)

3 tbsp oil

4 tbsp water

$1/4$ tsp sugar

$1/2$ tsp salt

REMPAH

10 shallots *(bawang merah)*

2 red chillies

3 candlenuts *(buah keras)*

1 tsp prawn (shrimp) paste
   (belacan)

PREPARATION

1 Prepare the water convolvulus. (See *Tips* below).

2 Prepare the *rempah*. Peel and roughly chop the shallots and chillies. Pound/blend together with the candlenuts and prawn paste.

METHOD

1 Heat a wok over a high flame until it smokes. Add the oil. Add the *rempah*, sugar and salt. Sprinkle some water to prevent it from burning. Stir-fry for about 5 min.

2 Add the water convolvulus and mix well with the *rempah*. Cook until the stems are tender but not overcooked.

Tips:

• To prepare the water convolvulus, cut off the roots, then thoroughly rinse. Pluck the leaves together with some stem to give the dish a crunchy texture.

• If it is prepared early, soak the leaves and stems in cold water then shake off the excess water before frying.

• For a variation of this dish, add 150 g of small, shelled fresh prawns just before adding the water convolvulus.

Otak-otak

Spicy fish cake wrapped and grilled in banana leaf

Suggested types of fish to use are Spanish mackerel *(ikan tenggiri)* or mackerel. Ask the fish monger to fillet and skin the fish for you. If you wish to do it yourself, 1 kg of fish will yield about 600 g minced fish. Small pieces of fish, prawn or cuttlefish should be added to the final mixture for additional texture. Otak-otak is best eaten with rice or bread.

INGREDIENTS

600 g minced fish (see page 142 for minced fish preparation)

150 ml water

3 or more onions

2 eggs

500 g grated coconut

240 ml water

1 tbsp sugar

1 tbsp salt

4 turmeric leaves *(daun kunyit)*

2 kaffir lime leaves *(daun limau purut)*

40 pieces banana leaves

80 toothpicks

REMPAH

1 thumb size knob turmeric *(kunyit)*

20 dried chillies

6 red chillies

25 slices galangal *(lengkuas)*

5 candlenuts *(buah keras)*

1 tbsp prawn (shrimp) paste *(belacan)*

PREPARATION

1 Soak the dried chillies for the *rempah* in hot water.

2 Peel and finely mince the onion. Finely slice the turmeric leaves and kaffir lime leaves. Set aside.

3 Prepare the coconut cream. (See page 185).

4 Prepare the *rempah*. Deseed then roughly chop the soaked and fresh chillies. Peel the turmeric and galangal. Very finely pound/blend all the *rempah* ingredients together.

5 Wipe the banana leaves clean, then blanch in boiling water or heat over an open flame to soften. Cut each leaf into 15 x 25 cm pieces.

METHOD

1 Place the minced fish in a large bowl. Add the water and beat well. Add the *rempah*, onions and eggs. Mix well and add the coconut cream, sugar, salt, turmeric leaves and kaffir lime leaves.

2 Place 1 tbsp of the mixture onto the centre of a banana leaf sheet. Fold the top and bottom third of the leaf over the mixture, then secure each open end with a toothpick. Alternatively, larger parcels of Otak-otak can be made by using 4 rounded tbsp of mixture. Place the mixture onto a larger piece of banana leaf then fold to seal the mixture in.

3 Place parcels over a charcoal grill and cook each side for 5 min, or grill in a preheated oven at 180°C for 5–7 min on each side.

Otak-otak Putih

Fish cake wrapped and grilled in banana leaf

Coconut leaves are also used to wrap *otak-otak* as shown in the picture on the right.

INGREDIENTS

600 g minced fish meat
2–3 egg whites
500 g grated coconut
4 tbsp water
³/₄ tbsp salt
a dash of pepper

40 pieces banana leaves
80 toothpicks

PREPARATION

1 To prepare the minced fish, fillet the fish. Skin the fish by running a sharp knife between the meat and skin. Run your fingers through the meat to remove any bones then finely mince the meat. To further remove any bones or impurities, press the minced fish meat through a sieve over a large bowl using the rounded end of a spoon or a pastry scrapper.

2 Prepare the coconut cream. (See page 185).

3 Wipe the banana leaves clean, then blanch in boiling water or heat over an open flame to soften. Cut each leaf into 15 x 25 cm pieces.

METHOD

1 Add the egg whites to the fish meat and beat well. Slowly add the coconut cream while beating continually. Add the salt and pepper and beat until smooth.

2 Place 1 tbsp of the mixture onto the centre of a banana leaf sheet. Fold the top and bottom third of the leaf over the mixture, then secure each open end with a toothpick.

3 Place the parcels over a charcoal grill, cooking it on each side for 5 min, or grill in a preheated oven at 180°C for 5–7 min on each side.

Sambal Timun

Cucumbers in *sambal*

This is usually served as a side dish with Nasi Lemak. It may also be served on its own. For a variation, simply add one small onion, one sliced chicken liver and gizzard (rinsed with salt, discard the fat and boil for 10 min, rinse in cold water then finely sliced) and three sprigs of chopped coriander (Chinese parsley).

INGREDIENTS

2 cucumbers

REMPAH

2 red chillies

1¹/₂ tbsp prawn (shrimp) paste (*belacan*)

4 tbsp dried prawns (shrimps) (*udang kering*)

MARINADE

2 tbsp sugar

2 tbsp vinegar

1 tbsp kalamansi lime *(limau kesturi)* or lemon juice

¹/₂ tsp salt

PREPARATION

1 Rinse then cut off the ends of the cucumbers. Rub the ends against the sliced surface to extract the bitterness. Cut the cucumbers into quarters lengthwise. Deseed, then slice diagonally.

2 Finely slice the chillies and deseed, if preferred.

3 Place the prawn paste in a toaster or in a dry pan. Toast for 3–5 min. Wrap in foil to prevent the smell from escaping.

4 Stir all the ingredients for the marinade together until the sugar and salt have dissolved.

5 Prepare the *rempah*. Pound/blend all the *rempah* ingredients together then mix in the marinade.

METHOD

1 Toss the prepared cucumbers and the *rempah* mixture together until well mixed. Serve or refrigerate.

Ikan Bilis

Whitebait and peanuts with caramelised sugar and chilli powder

This simple dish can be served as a snack or as a side dish with any Peranakan food.

INGREDIENTS

300 g dried whitebait
  (ikan bilis)
2 onions
180 ml oil
150 g peanuts, toasted
2 tbsp chilli powder
4 tbsp sugar

PREPARATION

1 Quickly rinse then shake the dried whitebait dry. Do not soak. Dry in the sun or oven-dry. (Drying the whitebait will ensure that the fish will be crisp when fried).

2 Peel then finely pound/blend the onions.

METHOD

1 Heat a wok over a high flame until it smokes. Add the oil. Reduce to a medium flame, then add the peanuts. Stir-fry until light golden brown. Remove and drain well.

2 Reheat the oil over a high flame, then add the dried whitebait. Stir-fry until light golden brown and crispy. Remove and drain.

3 Discard the used oil then wipe the wok clean.

4 Add some new oil. Stir-fry the onions for a few min.

5 Add the chilli powder and sugar. Stir-fry for a few min.

6 Lower to a medium flame then add the peanuts and whitebait. Toss together then remove.

7 Allow to cool before storing in an airtight container.

Lontong

Lontong originates from Indonesia. It is a variety of spicy dishes served with Nasi Tindeh. It includes Beef Rendang, Serondeng Beef, Opor Ayam, Sayur Lodeh, Tempe Goreng, Sambal Goreng Java, Egg Sambal, Achar and Emping. Other optional dishes include Beef Cutlet, Satay and Udang Asam Goreng.

Beef Rendang

Beef in a spicy coconut sauce

This recipe originates from Padang in West Sumatra, Indonesia, hence, the name Nasi Padang which is sometimes used to refer to such dishes.

INGREDIENTS

1 onion

600 g beef shin

500 g grated coconut

water

1 rounded tbsp tamarind (asam) pulp

1 tsp sugar

1 tsp salt

REMPAH

4 slices galangal (lengkuas)

4 slices ginger (halia)

4 cloves garlic (bawang putih)

15 dried chillies or 2 tbsp pounded red chillies

1 stalk lemon grass (serai)

1 tbsp coriander (ketumbar) powder

$^{1}/_{2}$ tsp cumin (jintan putih)

PREPARATION

1 Soak the dried chillies for the rempah in hot water.

2 Slice the beef into big or small pieces, depending on your preference.

3 Peel and slice the onion. Set aside.

4 Prepare the coconut milk using 570 ml water. (See page 185).

5 Prepare the tamarind marinade using 120 ml water. (See page 185).

6 Prepare the rempah. Deseed then roughly chop the soaked dried chillies. Peel and roughly slice the galangal, ginger and garlic. Pound/blend together with the coriander powder and cumin, adding the peeled and bruised lemon grass (use white portion only) last.

METHOD

1 Combine all the ingredients in a saucepan. Bring to the boil then simmer uncovered until the sauce has reduced by half. Cover and simmer for 30 min until the meat is tender.

Serondeng Beef

Beef with spice-flavoured grated coconut

INGREDIENTS

1 rounded tsp tamarind (asam) pulp

280 ml water

6 tbsp oil

600 g beef fillet

3 tbsp palm sugar (gula Melaka)

1 1/2 tsp salt

500 g grated coconut

REMPAH

2 stalks lemon grass (serai)

6 slices galangal (lengkuas)

4 slices ginger (halia)

1/2 thumb size knob turmeric (kunyit) or 1 tsp turmeric powder

2 tsp coriander (ketumbar) powder

1 tsp cumin (jintan putih) powder

PREPARATION

1　Prepare the tamarind marinade. (See page 185).

2　Prepare the *rempah*. Peel then roughly chop the lemon grass (use white portion only), galangal, ginger and turmeric. Finely pound/blend all the *rempah* ingredients together, adding the coriander and cumin powders last.

METHOD

1　Heat a wok over a high flame until it smokes. Add the oil. Lower the flame then stir-fry the *rempah* for a few seconds. Add the meat.

2　Once the meat is half-cooked, add the tamarind marinade, then the palm sugar and salt.

3　Simmer until very little of the gravy remains, then add the grated coconut. Stir-fry until the grated coconut is dry and brown.

Opor Ayam

Chicken stewed in a fragrant yellow coconut-based gravy

INGREDIENTS

1 whole chicken or 1 kg chicken pieces

1 stalk lemon grass *(serai)*

4 tbsp oil

500 g grated coconut

700 ml water

1 tbsp sugar

1 tbsp salt

2 kaffir lime leaves *(daun limau purut)*

REMPAH

2 red chillies

4 slices galangal *(lengkuas)*

2 slices ginger *(halia)*

4 candlenuts *(buah keras)*

15 shallots *(bawang merah)*

2 cloves garlic *(bawang putih)*

3 tsp coriander *(ketumbar)* powder

$1/2$ tsp cumin *(jintan putih)* powder

$1/2$ tsp pepper

1 tsp turmeric *(kunyit)* powder

Tip:

Use an aluminium or non-stick pan to prevent the coconut gravy from discolouring when cooking.

PREPARATION

1 If using a whole chicken, cut it into large pieces.

2 Peel off the outer layer of the lemon grass then bruise.

3 Prepare the coconut milk. (See page 185).

4 Prepare the *rempah*. Deseed (optional) then roughly chop the red chillies. Peel then roughly chop the galangal, ginger, shallots and garlic. Very finely pound/blend together with the candlenuts, adding the coriander, cumin, pepper and turmeric powders last.

METHOD

1 Heat a wok over a high flame until it smokes. Add the oil. Lower the flame then add the *rempah* and lemon grass. Stir-fry for 2 min. Add 3 tbsp coconut milk the stir-fry for 5 min more. Stir constantly for a smooth gravy.

2 Add the chicken and 6 tbsp coconut milk. Stir-fry for 5 min.

3 Over a high flame, add the remaining coconut milk, sugar, salt and kaffir lime leaves. Bring to the boil then simmer uncovered for about 20 min or until the chicken is cooked.

Sayur Lodeh

Stewed vegetables in coconut gravy, a dish of Indonesian origin

INGREDIENTS

300 g cooked bamboo shoots
  (rebung)
80 g Chinese cabbage
2 sticks dried yellow tofu skin
  (taukee)
160 g long beans
160 g French beans
160 g carrots
1 onion
600 g (2 pieces) firm tofu
  (taukua)
300 g (3 pieces) fermented soy
  bean cakes *(tempe)*
300 g small prawns (shrimps)
2 tbsp dried prawns (shrimps)
  (udang kering)
150 ml oil
500 g grated coconut
1 l water
1¹/₂ tsp sugar
1 tbsp salt

REMPAH

5 candlenuts *(buah keras)*
20 shallots *(bawang merah)*
2 cloves garlic *(bawang putih)*
10 dried chillies or 1 tbsp
  pounded chillies
1 tbsp prawn (shrimp) paste
  (belacan)
¹/₄ tsp turmeric *(kunyit)* powder
1 thumb size knob galangal
  (lengkuas)

PREPARATION

1 If dried chillies are used for the *rempah*, soak them in hot water.
2 Slice the bamboo shoots, cabbage and dried tofu skin into 2.5 cm squares.
3 Rinse then cut the long beans and French beans into 2.5 cm lengths.
4 Peel then slice the carrots and onion.
5 Cut the firm tofu and fermented soy bean cakes into small cubes or slices.
6 Shell and devein the small prawns (optional).
7 Roughly pound/chop the dried prawns.
8 Prepare the coconut milk. (See page 185).
9 Prepare the *rempah*. Deseed then roughly chop the soaked dried chillies, if using. Peel and roughly chop the shallots and garlic. Pound/blend all the *rempah* ingredients together, adding the turmeric powder and peeled and bruised galangal last.

METHOD

1 Heat a wok over a high flame until it smokes. Add the oil. Sit-fry the firm tofu pieces until light golden brown. Remove and drain.
2 Fry the fermented soy bean cakes until golden brown. Remove and drain.
3 Add the *rempah*, then lower the flame. Add the dried prawns and onions. Stir-fry.
4 Over a high flame, add the small prawns then stir-fry. Add 5 tbsp coconut milk and stir-fry for a few minutes.
5 Add the remaining vegetables and dried tofu skin. Fry for 5 min, then add the remaining coconut milk. Bring to the boil and continue stirring.
6 Add the fried fermented soy bean cakes and fried firm tofu. Simmer for 10–15 min. Add salt and sugar to taste.

Tempe Goreng

Fried fermented soy bean cakes and tofu glazed in a spicy sauce

INGREDIENTS

400 g (4 pieces) fermented soy bean cakes *(tempe)*

400 g (2 pieces) firm tofu *(taukua)*

200 g prawns (shrimps)

10 shallots *(bawang merah)*

8 cloves garlic *(bawang putih)*

6 green chillies

3 red chillies

4 dried chillies

2 stalks lemon grass *(serai)*

1 rounded tbsp tamarind *(asam)* pulp

120 ml water

150 ml oil

2 tsp sugar

2 tsp salt

PREPARATION

1 Cut the fermented soy bean cakes and firm tofu into small cubes.

2 Shell and devein the prawns. (Freeze the shells for use in other recipes).

3 Peel and slice the shallots and garlic.

4 Slice the chillies and deseed, if preferred.

5 Soak the dried chillies in hot water, deseed, if preferred, then pound.

6 Peel then slice the lemon grass (use white portion only).

7 Prepare the tamarind marinade. (See page 185).

METHOD

1 Heat a wok over a high flame until it smokes. Add the oil. Stir-fry the fermented tofu cubes, then the firm tofu cubes. Remove and drain.

2 In the same oil, stir-fry the shallots, then add the garlic, lemon grass and fresh chillies. Stir-fry for 1 min, then add the pounded dried chillies, sugar and salt. Stir-fry for another minute before adding the prawns and tamarind marinade.

3 When the prawns are cooked, add the fried firm tofu cubes and the fried fermented tofu cubes. Mix well then serve.

Sambal Goreng Java

Prawns and eggs in a coconut gravy

INGREDIENTS

300 g small prawns (shrimps)

20 quail eggs or 3 chicken eggs

3 red chillies

3 green chillies

6 shallots *(bawang merah)*

4 cloves garlic *(bawang putih)*

2 slices galangal *(lengkuas)*

5 tbsp oil

1 tsp pounded chilli
  (use fresh or dried chillies)

125 g grated coconut

180 ml water

1¹/₂ tsp sugar

1 tsp salt

> **Tip:**
> Use an aluminum or non-stick pan to prevent the coconut gravy from discolouring when cooking.

PREPARATION

1 Shell and devein the prawns (optional).

2 Hardboil then peel the eggs.

3 Slice the chillies diagonally and deseed (if preferred).

4 Peel then slice the shallots, garlic and galangal.

5 Prepare the coconut milk. (See page 185).

METHOD

1 Heat a wok over a high flame until it smokes. Add the oil. Lower the flame then add the shallots, garlic and galangal. Stir-fry.

2 Add the fresh chillies and pounded chilli then the prawns.

3 Once the prawns are half-cooked, add the coconut milk. Lower the flame, then add the eggs, sugar and salt. Simmer for a few minutes, stirring occasionally.

Egg Sambal

Hardboiled eggs in a spicy tomato based sauce

INGREDIENTS

30 quail eggs or 10 chicken eggs
125 g grated coconut
120 ml water
5 tbsp oil
5 tbsp tomato paste
1 tsp lime or lemon juice
3 tsp sugar
1 tsp salt

REMPAH

1 slice ginger *(halia)*
12 shallots *(bawang merah)*
1 clove garlic *(bawang putih)*
1 tsp chilli powder

PREPARATION

1   In a large pot, hardboil then shell the eggs.

2   Prepare the coconut milk. (See page 185).

3   Prepare the *rempah*. Peel and roughly chop the ginger, shallots and garlic. Pound/blend all the *rempah* ingredients together, adding the chilli powder last.

METHOD

1   Heat a wok over a high flame until it smokes. Add the oil. Stir-fry the *rempah* for 1 min then add the tomato paste then stir-fry for another 1 min. Add the eggs and stir-fry for 1 min, then add the coconut milk.

2   Simmer for a few min before adding the lime or lemon juice, sugar and salt. Simmer for another 3–5 min until the gravy has thickened.

Sayur Ketupat

Sayur Ketupat comprises Nasi Tindeh (cubes of rice) served with a selection of vegetables cooked in *sambal* or any spicy gravy including Sambal Kacang Panjang, Sambal Belimbing, Sambal Kangkung Santan and Sambal Gerago.

Nasi Tindeh

Cubes of compressed of rice served with a variety of dishes

Nasi Tindeh is often served with Lontong, Satay or the Sayur Ketupat dishes in the following pages.

INGREDIENTS

600 g rice or broken rice
  (*beras hancur*)
2.3 l water

METHOD

1 Bring the rice and water to the boil, then simmer until more than half of the water has evaporated. Stir the rice thoroughly until it has a smooth consistency. Cook over a low flame until dry.

2 Line a bowl with a sheet of muslin cloth twice the size of the bowl. Pour the rice into the bowl, then cover with the edges of the muslin.

3 Compress the rice by placing a slightly smaller bowl on top with a heavy object to weigh it down. Alternatively, use two flat trays.

4 Set aside for 8 hours at room temperature. Cut the rice into small cubes using a sharp wet knife.

Sambal Kacang Panjang

Prawns and long beans served in a spicy gravy

INGREDIENTS

160 g small prawns (shrimps)

300 g long beans

3 tbsp oil

125 g grated coconut

120 ml water

1 tsp sugar

1¹/₂ tsp salt

REMPAH

4 candlenuts *(buah keras)*

10 shallots *(bawang merah)*

2 red chillies

1 tsp prawn (shrimp) paste
   (belacan)

PREPARATION

1 Shell and devein the small prawns (optional).

2 Cut the long beans into 2.5 cm lengths. Blanch in boiling water with ¹/₂ tbsp soda bicarbonate (to help retain the colour).

3 Prepare the coconut milk. (See page 185).

4 Prepare the *rempah*. Peel then roughly chop the shallots. Pound/blend all the *rempah* ingredients together.

METHOD

1 Heat a wok over a high flame until it smokes. Add the oil. Add the *rempah* and stir-fry for about 3 min.

2 Add the prawns and about half the coconut milk. Stir-fry for a few min, then add the long beans. Add the remaining coconut milk and simmer for 2 min. Add sugar and salt to taste.

Sambal Belimbing

Prawns and bilimbi served in a spicy sauce

INGREDIENTS

300 g bilimbi fruit *(belimbing asam)*

300 g small prawns (shrimps)

5 tbsp oil

125 g grated coconut

120 ml water

4 tsp sugar

2 tsp salt

GARNISHES

5 shallots *(bawang merah)*

5 cloves garlic *(bawang putih)*

1 stalk lemon grass *(serai)*

REMPAH

4 candlenuts *(buah keras)*

10 shallots *(bawang merah)*

2 red chillies

1 tsp prawn (shrimp) paste *(belacan)*

PREPARATION

1 Rinse then slice the bilimbi.

2 Shell and devein the small prawns (optional).

3 Prepare the coconut milk. (See page 185).

4 Peel all the shallots and the garlic. Finely slice 5 shallots for the garnish and roughly chop the rest for the *rempah*.

5 Peel then slice the lemon grass (use white portion only).

6 Prepare the *rempah*. Roughly chop the chillies. Pound/blend all the *rempah* ingredients together.

METHOD

1 Heat a wok over a high flame until it smokes. Add the oil. Stir-fry the garnishes until golden brown. Remove and set aside.

2 Fry the *rempah*, then add 2 tbsp coconut milk. Add the prawns and bilimbi.

3 Stir-fry for 2–3 min then add the remaining coconut milk, sugar and salt. Simmer until cooked.

4 Place into a serving dish and garnish with fried shallots, garlic and lemon grass.

Sambal Kangkung Santan

Prawns and water convolvulus in a spicy coconut gravy

INGREDIENTS

1 kg water convolvulus
   (kangkung)
160 g small prawns (shrimps)
5 tbsp oil
125 g grated coconut
120 ml water
2 tsp sugar
1 tsp salt

REMPAH

6 candlenuts (buah keras)
15 shallots (bawang merah)
2 red chillies
1/2 tbsp prawn (shrimp) paste
   (belacan)

PREPARATION

1 Rinse and pluck the tender portions of the water convolvulus. (See page 138 for preparation details).

2 Shell and devein the prawns (optional).

3 Prepare the coconut milk. (See page 185).

4 Prepare the rempah. Peel and roughly chop the shallots. Pound/blend all the rempah ingredients together.

METHOD

1 Heat a wok over a high flame until it smokes. Add the oil. Lower the flame then stir-fry the rempah.

2 Add the prawns and 2 tbsp of coconut milk. Simmer for 2–3 min, then add the remaining coconut milk, sugar, salt and water convolvulus. Stir-fry for 2–3 min (do not overcook).

Sambal Gerago

Crisp tiny prawns with spices

INGREDIENTS

100 g tiny prawns (shrimps) *(udang gerago)*

2 kaffir lime leaves *(daun limau purut)*

125 g grated coconut

$^1/_2$ tsp coriander *(ketumbar)* powder

a pinch of chilli power

4 tsp sugar

$^1/_2$ tsp pepper

> **Tip:**
> Tiny prawns *(udang gerago)* can be substituted with 8 tbsp of pounded dried prawns *(udang kering)*.

PREPARATION

1 Rinse and drain the prawns. Leave in the sun to dry or in the oven at a low temperature.

2 Finely shred the kaffir lime leaves.

METHOD

1 Mix all the ingredients together.

2 Over a low flame in a dry pan with no oil, stir-fry the prawns until crisp. Allow to cool before storing in an airtight container.

Glossary

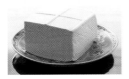

Soft Tofu *(Tauhu)*
Soft tofu has a soft silky texture and is used in a wide variety of savoury dishes. It tends to break apart easily so handle with care and do not overcook. Keep refrigerated and discard after 2–3 days or once it smells off. Drain excess water before using.

Firm Tofu *(Taukua),* **large and small pieces**
Firm tofu has a hard, rough texture and retains its shape and texture during cooking. Widely used in Peranakan and Asian cuisine, it is very versatile and can be boiled, steamed or fried, and it takes on the flavour of the dish it is cooked in readily. To store freshly made tofu from the wet market, change the water it is soaked in daily and drain the excess water before using. For the vacuum-packed tofu from the supermarket, open the packet only when required. Keep refrigerated and discard if not used after 2–3 days or once it smells off.

Dried Sweet Tofu Slices
(Tiam Taukee or *Teem Chok)*
Brown in colour, these sweetened hard dried tofu slices are often used in vegetarian cooking.

Fermented Soy Bean Cakes
(Tempe)
Although the presence of mould on fermented soy bean cakes is a little off-putting, it is what gives this ingredient its unique flavour. Commonly used in Malay and Indonesian cuisine, *tempe* is also used in Peranakan cooking.

Salted Soy Beans
(Taucheo), **whole**
These soy beans are a key ingredient in Peranakan cuisine. They are salty and have a strong but pleasant flavour. They are usually pounded slightly to make a smooth paste. Minced salted soy beans are also available in stores. Refrigerate after opening.

Chinese Sausage
(Lap Cheong)
This is a dried sweet smoky flavoured pork sausage commonly used in Cantonese cuisine. It is used in the popular Peranakan dish, Popiah. Steam, boil or fry before eating. Best stored in a cool, dry place or in the freezer.

Peanut Candy
(Gula Kacang)
Peanut candy is usually eaten as a snack and is sometimes used in *achar* recipes. If it is not available, pour caramelised sugar over roasted peanuts on a non-stick surface. Leave to harden and use as required.

Fresh Thick Rice Vermicelli
(Laksa *Beehoon*)
Made from rice flour, thick rice vermicelli keeps well for 2–3 days if refrigerated. Rinse before using. Substitutes: spaghetti or dried thin rice vermicelli.

Yellow Noodles
(Hokkien Mee)
Made from egg and wheat flour, rinse these noodles before using. Fresh egg noodles can keep for 2–3 days if refrigerated. Substitute: spaghetti.

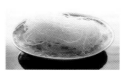

Glass Noodles
(Tunghoon)
Glass noodles become translucent once cooked, hence its name. Made from mung bean flour, it is also known as mung bean or cellophane noodles. Soak before using.

Rice Vermicelli *(Beehoon)*
Made from rice flour, these dried thin white noodles are usually added to soups or stir-fried. It is available at most supermarkets and wet markets. Soak before using.

Turmeric Leaves
(Daun Kunyit)
These long, wide leaves of the turmeric plant are commonly used in Indonesian curry dishes. Tearing or finely slicing them releases their flavour.

Mint Leaves
(Daun Pudina)
These dark green leaves impart a refreshing flavour to dishes. Sold in small bundles, any excess mint leaves can be stored in a plastic bag in the refrigerator for up to a few days.

Kaffir Lime Leaves
(Daun Limau Purut)
A distinctive leaf because it has two leaves joined end to end. It is usually used whole in curries or finely sliced to release its lovely citrus aroma. It keeps well frozen in a sealed bag.

Pink Ginger Buds
(Bunga Siantan)
These beautiful pink buds of the ginger plant are usually finely sliced then added to curries or the Indonesian salad, Rojak. It is aromatic and has a subtle but distinctive flavour.

Kalamansi Limes
(Limau Kesturi)
Smaller and deeper green in colour than ordinary lime, kalamansi limes are often used as a garnish. Its juice adds sourness to dishes and tenderises and preserves meat. Substitutes: lime or lemon.

Screwpine *(Pandan)*
Leaves *(Daun Pandan)*
The long, dark, green leaves of this plant are used in both savoury and sweet dishes for its distinct flavour and colour. Tie the leaf into a knot to make it easier to cook with and remove before serving. To extract the juice, pound or blend with a little water, then strain using muslin.

Lemon Grass *(Serai)*
To use this pale green, fibrous herb, peel away the first layer of leaves then bruise or slice to release its refreshing lemony aroma. Use the white bulbous portion and discard the green upper stalk. If used whole, remove before serving. Substitute: lemon peel.

Banana Bud
(Jantung Pisang)
The purple coloured banana 'bud' is also sometimes called the 'heart'. It is commonly used in curries and salads. It is very difficult to locate although some wet markets such as the Geylang Serai and Tekka markets will have them.

Coriander (Chinese Parsley)
(Daun Ketumbar)
Used as a garnish, the stems have a stronger, more pungent flavour compared to the leaves. Chop or tear to release its flavours. Store wrapped in newspapers or a plastic bag and refrigerate for up to a few days.

Chives *(Ku Chai)*
These long green and flat leaves have a subtle onion-like flavour. They are often chopped up into shorter lengths and used in dishes such as Mee Siam.

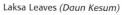

Laksa Leaves *(Daun Kesum)*
Characterised by narrow, pointed leaves which release a very delicate aromatic scent, this herb is commonly known as laksa leaf *(daun laksa)* since it is a key ingredient in the popular dish, Laksa.

Spring Onion (Scallion)
A young onion with an immature bulb, the spring onion has round hollow leaves and a mild flavour. It is commonly used to garnish cooked dishes.

Shallots *(Bawang Merah)*
A key ingredient in Peranakan cuisine, shallots are typically used pounded in *rempahs* or sliced and fried. Soaking makes it easier to remove the thin skin. Peel away from the eyes to avoid tearing. Substitute: onions.

Dried Chinese Mushrooms
Commonly used in both Chinese and Peranakan cooking. Soak in hot water to soften then squeeze out the excess water before using. Dried Chinese mushrooms store well for months in a clean airtight container.

Cloud/Wood Ear Fungus *(Boh Jee/Kuping Tikus)*
Commonly used in Chinese cooking but less so in Peranakan cooking, soak in hot water to soften before squeezing dry and using. It has a subtle flavour and crunchy texture. Stores well for months in a clean airtight container.

Dried Fish Bladder/Maw *(Hee Peow)*
This ingredient has a spongy texture and bland taste. It is mostly used in Chinese soups. To reconstitute, soak in hot water, squeeze dry then cut into pieces. It keeps well for months in a dry airtight container.

Dried Salted Fish
Fish is salted and dried to preserve and intensify its flavour across Asia. Small pieces are often used in soups or stir-fried with vegetables. It keeps well for months in a dry airtight container or in the freezer.

Prawn (Shrimp) Paste *(Belacan)*
This fermented paste is a key ingredient in Peranakan and Southeast Asian cuisine. Sold in blocks, prawn paste varies in terms of quality, texture and colour. It is extremely pungent but has a wonderful flavour.

Fresh Grated Coconut
Fresh grated coconut is used for its cream/milk and also in its grated form. Two types of grated coconut are available—black and white. The black variety is grated with the dark coconut skin while the white variety is skinned before grating. Use the white variety for dessert toppings and the black for extracting coconut cream/milk. Fresh grated coconut can be stored in the freezer. Thaw for about 1 hr before using or add hot water. For dishes that are less rich, use diluted coconut milk or substitute with skimmed or soy milk. Substitutes: pasteurised coconut cream or milk, powdered or desiccated coconut.

Tiny Dried Prawns (Shrimps) *(Udang Gerago)*
These tiny dried prawns (shrimps) keep for months in a dry airtight container or in the freezer and are also available as a thick pungent sauce known as *cencaluk*.

Dried Prawns (Shrimps) *(Udang Kering)*
These salted, dried prawns are frequently used in Peranakan cuisine, especially in *rempahs*. They keep well for months in a dry airtight container or in the freezer.

Dried Whitebait *(Ikan Bilis)*
Tiny dried fish which are usually deep-fried and eaten as a snack or side dish, or used to enrich stocks. Keeps for months in a dry airtight container or in the freezer.

Salted Radish *(Chai Po)*
Made from radish preserved in spices and salt, salted radish is usually sold in packets at the wet market, local supermarkets or Chinese grocers.

White Sesame Seeds *(Bijan)*
Sesame seeds have a wonderful nutty flavour and aroma. They can be eaten raw although the flavour is best when toasted.

Candlenuts *(Buah Keras)*
This waxy nut is pounded in *rempahs* and used as a thickening agent. Substitutes: macadamia nuts, almonds, hazelnuts or Brazil nuts (skinned).

Quail Eggs
These small speckled eggs are used in both sweet and savory Peranakan and Asian dishes. Use as you normally would chicken eggs.

Palm Sugar *(Gula Melaka)*
This unrefined sugar has a rich caramelised flavour. Sold in cylindrical blocks, slice or grate the amount you require. It is typically used in Peranakan, Malay and Indonesian cooking. Substitutes: brown or muscovado sugar.

Star Anise
(Pekek/Bunga Lawang)
This star-shaped spice is widely used in Asian cuisine and is usually added to curries and stocks whole. It releases a strong aromatic woody flavour that goes well with meat dishes.

Nutmeg *(Buah Pala)*
This small dried seed has a strong and distinctive taste. Grate in small amounts to season dishes. Whole dried nutmegs are not commonly sold in Singapore, although it originates from this region. Substitute: nutmeg powder.

Cassia Bark *(Kayu Manis)*
Often mistaken for cinnamon, an easy way to identify cassia is that the quills tend to have a frayed edge. It releases an aromatic woody flavour when cooked. Remove before serving. Substitutes: cinnamon or cinnamon powder.

Cinnamon Sticks
Although similar in aroma and texture to cassia, cinnamon sticks are slightly thicker and typically have a straighter edge. Use the same way you would cassia. Remove before serving. Substitute: cinnamon powder.

Bird's Eye Chillies *(Cili Padi)*
As a rule of thumb, the smaller the chilli, the more intense the heat. This chilli is certainly much spicier than normal red chillies. (*Cili padi* is also a local term of endearment for someone who has a fiery personality!)

Buah Keluak Meat
This dense dark-coloured flesh of the *buah keluak* nut, an Indonesian black nut, is also available pre-packed at wet markets. If unavailable, extract the meat by cracking open the whole nut. *Buah keluak* meat keeps well in a cool dry place or in the refrigerator.

Buah Keluak Nut
This large brown nut is widely grown in Indonesia and is poisonous when raw. It is difficult to find in markets outside of Southeast Asia and its unique texture and flavour means that there is no substitute for it. Soak the black nuts for 24 hr and brush them clean before using.

Fresh Tamarind *(Asam)*
Fresh tamarind comes in a long brown pod. Remove the pod and seeds before using. Fresh tamarind has a less intense flavour compared to tamarind *(asam)* pulp, so use more if necessary. Store in the refrigerator for up to a few weeks. Substitute: tamarind pulp.

Tamarind *(Asam)* **Pulp**
This thick brown pulp is a key ingredient in Peranakan cuisine. Do not store in a metal container since tamarind is highly acidic and therefore corrosive. Instead, store in earthen pots or plastic bags. Tamarind pulp does not require refrigeration and keeps well for months. Substitute: fresh tamarind *(asam)* or dried sour fruit slices *(asam gelugur)*.

Dried Chillies
These are dried red chillies. They are used for their earthy deep red colour. Remove the stems (if any) then soak in hot water to soften before using. Deseed if you prefer your dish less spicy. One way is to slit the chilli then shake the seeds out before soaking, although not all the seeds will fall out. Alternatively, soak to soften then slice in half and scrap the seeds away using the edge of a sharp knife, as you would fresh chillies. Substitute: chilli powder.

Turmeric *(Kunyit)*
The vibrant yellow-orange colour and distinctive taste of this rhizome adds colour and enhances the flavour of dishes, even when used in small amounts. Be careful when cooking with turmeric as it stains. Peel before using. Turmeric is traditionally measured by slices or thumb size (1 thumb size = 5 cm). Substitute: turmeric powder.

Galangal *(Lengkuas)*
Also known as blue ginger, galangal has a brownish-pink skin and pale yellow flesh. It is one of the key ingredients in Peranakan cuisine and defines it with its unique flavour and aroma. Galangal is traditionally measured by slices or thumb size (1 thumb size = 5 cm). Substitute: galangal powder.

Ginger *(Halia)*
This rhizome has a light brown skin and cream-coloured flesh. It is a key ingredient in Peranakan and Asian cuisine. Peel before using. Ginger is traditionally measured by slices or thumb size (1 thumb size = 5 cm). Substitute: ginger powder.

Fresh Red/Green Chillies
Red chillies are commonly used in *rempahs*. The 'heat' comes from the seeds, so adjust the intensity by deseeding accordingly. To deseed, slice in half then scrap the seeds away with a knife. The recipes in this cookbook have been adjusted to a moderate spiciness. Use gloves when preparing chillies and avoid contact with your eyes. Substitute: chilli powder. Green chillies are unripened chillies and are mostly used as a garnish for its vibrant green colour.

Chilli Flakes
Mince dried red chillies to obtain chilli flakes.

Chilli Powder
This powdered version of dried red chillies is used for its colour and to add spice to dishes.

Ginger *(Halia)* Powder
Although fresh ginger is typically used in Peranakan cuisine, this powdered form is a good substitute.

Cinnamon Powder
Cinnamon powder is a good substitute for cinnamon sticks or cassia if both are unavailable.

Nutmeg *(Buah Pala)* Powder
This powdered version of the nutmeg releases a strong flavour and should be used in small amounts.

Cumin *(Jintan Putih)* Powder
Cumin powder is ground from cumin seeds. To prepare your own, dry-roast cumin seeds then pound.

Cloves *(Bunga Cengkih)*
A strong spice with a woody aroma, cloves are used to a limited extent in Peranakan cuisine. Use whole and in small amounts.

Fennel *(Jintan Manis)* Powder
This is the dried and ground version of fennel seeds. To prepare your own, dry-roast fennel seeds then pound.

Coriander *(Ketumbar)*
These tiny light brown pods release a strong and distinctive aroma and are a key ingredient in Peranakan cuisine.

Coriander *(Ketumbar)* Powder
This is the dried and ground version of coriander seeds. To prepare your own, dry-roast coriander pods then pound.

Cumin *(Jintan Putih)*
These tiny long dark brown seeds release a wonderfully rich aroma and are a key spice in Peranakan and South Asian cuisine. Cumin is sold in seed or powdered form in small bottles at the supermarket, or in small packets from spice sellers at the wet market. They look very similar to fennel seeds, but cumin seeds are darker in colour and slightly thinner.

Bitter Nut (Melinjo) Crackers *(Emping)*, dried and fried
Made from the bitter nut, these crackers have a slight bitter taste. Prepare in the same way as you would prawn crackers. Perfect as a snack or eaten with dishes such as Gado Gado.

Prawn Crackers *(Keropok)*, dried and fried
Traditionally made of minced prawn meat mixed with flour and spices, most commercially available ones nowadays do not contain meat, but just prawn flavouring. It is usually served as a snack or with Lontong and curries. Sun dry or dry in the oven using low heat, then fry in oil until it has fully expanded. Drain well then allow to cool before storing in an airtight container.

Caul Lining
This lacy translucent net is from the abdominal cavity of pigs and sheep. Since it is rarely used, only some butchers would be able to provide it and are likely to do so for free as it is usually discarded. Caul lining is used to wrap minced meat to enhance the flavour and keep the meat moist. The fatty membrane melts and becomes transparent when cooked.

Long Beans

These thin long green-coloured pods are so-named because they grow to be very long. The soft crunchy texture makes long beans ideal for salads, curries and stews. Substitute: French beans.

Chinese Radish *(Lobak)*

This long white root is often used in soups and stews. Peel the skin away before using.

Okra (Ladies' Fingers)

This long green-coloured vegetable resembles human fingers, hence its name. Use whole or sliced in stir-fries or curries.

French Beans

These long green-coloured pods have a soft crunchy texture, making them ideal for stir-fries, salads and pickles. Substitute: long beans.

Fresh Mustard Cabbage *(Kai Choi)*

The broad and large leaves of this cabbage are typically used in Asian cuisine for soups or stir-fries. It has a strong mustard-like flavour, hence its name.

Eggplant (Aubergine/ Brinjal)

Although eggplants come in a variety of shapes and sizes, the local variety is slender, long and light purple in colour. It has white flesh and little brown seeds. Used mainly in stir-fries or curries.

Water Convolvulus *(Kangkung)*

Known locally as *kangkung*, this is a tasty vegetable that is often cooked at home and at restaurants. Rinse thoroughly before using. Discard the roots and pluck off the leafy parts, retaining some of the stem which add crunch. Substitute: spinach.

Banana Leaves *(Daun Pisang)*

Widely used across Asia to wrap sweet and savoury food before cooking to impart a subtle aroma to the dish, while making it aesthetically more pleasing. It is also used as a disposable, organic 'plate'. Wipe thoroughly with a damp cloth before using.

Salam Leaves *(Daun Salam)*

Largely similar in shape and size to the bay leaf, these dark green leaves are used whole in soups and curries to impart a unique flavour to the dish. They can be used fresh or dried. Omit if unavailable.

Bilimbi *(Belimbing Asam)*

This small fruit has a waxy green skin and a very sharp sour taste. Although not commonly found in markets, it grows easily in the tropics. It is typically used in salads and pickles.

Local Lettuce *(Sayur Salad)*

Local lettuce has a curly edge, soft crunchy texture and subtle taste. It is commonly served with spring rolls, used in salads or as a garnish. Substitutes: butter or romaine lettuce.

Bean Sprouts *(Tauge)*
With the growing popularity of Asian cuisine, bean sprouts are now found in most supermarkets in major cities. Although commercially sold bean sprouts are usually tailed, some still come with their hard dark green caps and brown roots. Pluck these off by hand as desired.

Bamboo Shoot *(Rebung)*
Bamboo shoots are sold raw or pre-cooked. Pre-cooked ones are available in cans and vacuum packs. For raw bamboo shoots, remove the hard outer layer then simmer until tender. This will take about 20 min, depending on the size of the piece.

Salted Cabbage *(Kiam Chai)*
It has a crunchy texture and is very salty but keeps well for months in its brine. Usually sold vacuum-packed or bottled at the wet market, supermarket or Chinese grocer. Rinse or soak for a few minutes before using to remove some, but not all, of the salt.

Dried Yellow Tofu Skin *(Taukee* or *Fu Chok)*
Thin dried sheets of tofu are obtained from coagulated soy bean milk. Often used in desserts and in savoury dishes. Soak in cold water to soften before use.

Turnip (Yam Bean/*Bang Kuang)*
Turnips have an earthy brown skin and crisp white-coloured flesh that can be eaten raw or cooked. Scrub away the soil then peel off the skin before using.

Dried Lily Buds *(Kim Chiam)*
These light brown buds are often used in stews and salads. It is sometimes knotted before use. Dried lily buds keep well in a clean airtight container.

Essential Ingredients for the Nonya Kitchen

Basics

Oil

Pepper

Salt

Sugar

Vinegar (e.g. white vinegar
or rice wine vinegar)

Spices

Cassia (*kayu manis*)

Chilli powder, dried chillies,
fresh red chillies

Cloves (*bunga cengkih*) (optional)

Coriander (*ketumbar*) powder

Cumin (*jintan putih*) powder

Fennel (*jintan manis*) powder

Garlic (*bawang putih*)

Onions

Shallots (*bawang merah*)

Star anise (*pepek/bunga lawang*)
(optional)

Tumeric (*kunyit*) powder

Dried Ingredients

Candlenuts (*buah keras*)

Dried whitebait (*ikan bilis*)

Dried Chinese mushrooms

Dried prawns (shrimps)
(*udang kering*)

Palm sugar (*gula Melaka*)

Rice

Preserved Ingredients

Pasteurised coconut milk/powder

Prawn (shrimp) paste (*belacan*)

Salted soy beans (*taucheo*)

Tamarind (*asam*) pulp

Basic Cooking Techniques

***Rempah* is the Malay term for spices pounded together.**

How to Prepare *Rempah*

1 Prepare all the *rempah* ingredients as listed in the recipe. Soak the dried chillies in hot water to soften (about 15 min). Peel and roughly chop ingredients such as shallots, ginger, turmeric and galangal. Deseed the chillies to make them less spicy, if desired, then roughly chop.

2 Using a mortar and pestle, start by pounding the hardest ingredients first or follow the order laid out in the recipe.

3 Gradually add the remaining ingredients, pounding to a desired consistency each time. The timing as to when each ingredient is to be added and how long pounding is required is a matter of judgment which comes with practice and experience. Pounding for too long or too short a period will result in an uneven consistency or incorrect texture.

4 Continue to pound until the desired texture (course, fine or very fine) is attained. Use as required.

Note:

1 The main difference between pounding by hand and using an electric blender is that pounding by hand gives you better control of the texture, resulting in a better quality *rempah*. The pounding action not only minces the pulp but releases the juices. The blender minces up the ingredients, often too finely, and sometimes water or oil needs to be added for the blender to work smoothly. Although pounding is preferable, for practical purposes, it is acceptable to use a blender.

2 Getting a rhythm to pounding is key since this will result in a more even consistency.

3 Always angle the pestle slightly when pounding so that the ingredients stay in the centre of the mortar. This will result in an even texture.

How to Prepare Coconut Cream/Milk

1 Place the grated coconut into a large bowl then pour water over it. Leave it to soak for a few minutes. The exact amounts of grated coconut and water are listed in the individual recipes.

2 Spoon the pulp into a muslin bag or clean kitchen towel.

3 Over a bowl, twist the bag/towel then squeeze down to extract the coconut cream/milk.

4 Alternatively, squeeze a handful of the pulp with your fingers, over a sieve. This would be considered the first extraction. For a second extraction, repeat the process again. Finally, discard the used grated coconut.

Note:

1 The difference between coconut cream and coconut milk is that coconut cream is obtained from the first extraction using very little water.

2 The first extraction will result in a coconut cream or a thicker, richer coconut milk, depending on the amount of water used. The second extraction will result in a more diluted coconut milk.

3 When boiling coconut milk, stir continuously and do not overboil, or it will *pecah minyak* (split). This means it will curdle and the coconut oil will separate.

4 A little salt is sometimes added to grated coconut or coconut cream/milk to enhance its flavour and preserve it.

5 Grated coconut and dishes cooked using coconut milk will spoil easily, so keep them refrigerated. Discard fresh grated coconut after 1–2 days in the refrigerator or keep frozen.

How to Prepare Tamarind Marinade

1 In a bowl, combine the tamarind and water according to the amount listed in the recipe.

2 Using your fingers, rub the tamarind pulp off the seeds.

3 Strain the mixture through a sieve. Discard the seeds. Use as required.

Basic Kitchen Equipment

Perforated Ladle

- Ideal for scooping up and draining food.

Rounded Ladle

- Rounded ladles are ideal for scooping out and serving anything with a lot of liquid.
- More experienced and traditional chefs also use it to measure quantities of liquid such as oil, water or stock. One ladleful is equivalent to about 5 tbsp.

'Cooking' Chopsticks

- Compared to ordinary table chopsticks, these chopsticks are thicker and extra long. They are perfect for frying and tossing noodles.

Wok Ladle

- The wok ladle is one of the most commonly used instruments in Asian cooking. It is used for stir-frying, tossing, lifting and scooping.
- The slightly rounded edge of the wok ladle fits the contours of the wok perfectly.

Mortar and Pestle *(Batu Lesung)*

- This mortar and pestle pictured here is the same one that was illustrated in the original edition of *Mrs Lee's Cookbook*. It has been in my family for at least 40 years and was used by my grandmother.
- To season a mortar and pestle, use it to pound some sand. Discard the sand then pound some vegetable remnants. Discard the pounded vegetable remnants and repeat the process twice. Finally, pound some raw rice until it is fine. Discard the rice and repeat this process until the mortar and pestle are smooth and the pounded rice is white in colour.

Wok *(Kuali)*

- There are various types of woks: iron, steel and non-stick. Iron woks are preferable since they can last for decades and get better with age. Woks are extremely versatile. They can be used for frying, steaming, boiling, braising and toasting.

- A well-seasoned wok will enhance the taste of the food cooked in it. If well taken care of, a wok can be passed down generations like a family heirloom. This one pictured here is at least 40 years old, if not more. It is the wok that my grandmother cooked with. It continues to be used in my home today and was used to cook the dishes in this cookbook.

- Iron woks need to be seasoned before use. The traditional method my grandmother used was to fry the pulp of a grated coconut until dry. Discard the pulp then quickly rinse the wok. Next, halve an onion and rub it on the inner surface of the wok. Roughly chop the onion, then heat 2 tbsp of oil in the wok and fry the chopped onion. Discard the onion and oil. Wipe it clean then coat it with a layer of clean oil. Repeat this process if necessary.

- A common way to remove burnt food is by soaking the wok in water until the residue comes off. If necessary, scrub the burnt area, wash with soap, rinse, dry then coat with a layer of clean oil.

- Avoid scrubbing the wok with anything abrasive, unless removing burnt food, and always coat it with a layer of clean oil after use to prevent rusting.

- Enamel and non-stick woks do not require seasoning and are generally easier to cook with, but be careful not to scratch the surface. Avoid using metal ladles and discard the wok once the surface is scratched.

Steamer

- Steamers offer an efficient and healthy way of cooking. While blanching or boiling food, particularly vegetables, causes nutrients and flavours to be lost, this is less so with steaming. I use the steamer when there are a number of ingredients I need to cook separately, for example when preparing Popiah. The top section can be used to steam vegetables, while the bottom section can be used to boil eggs.
- I use this particular enamel steamer for steaming Nasi Lemak because the small holes in the steamer basket prevents the rice from falling through.

Chinese Cleaver

- The Chinese cleaver is extremely versatile. It can be used for slicing, crushing, mincing, tenderising and scrapping. It is my favourite piece of kitchen equipment because, like the wok, it is simple in its construct but has a wide range of uses. With practice and some skill, it can be used to deftly slice fine sheets of tofu or cut a whole chicken into pieces in a matter of seconds.
- To slice: hold the cleaver firmly in one hand. With the other hand, place it firmly on the ingredient then curl your fingers. Lean the flat side of the cleaver against your knuckles and proceed to slice using an upward and downward motion.
- To crush: hold the cleaver firmly in one hand. Lay the flat end of the cleaver onto the ingredient then press firmly with the other hand. Alternatively, smash the blade flat against the ingredient. This is the easiest way to remove the skin off of a clove of garlic or bruise a piece of lemon grass or turmeric.
- To mince: hold the cleaver firmly in one hand and repeatedly chop across a piece of meat/vegetable then fold it over by lifting it with the blade. This is perfect for mincing tofu, fish or pork. Garlic/shallots can also be roughly or finely minced using this same method.
- To tenderise: hold the cleaver firmly in one hand with the blunt edge of the blade facing down. Repeatedly chop across a piece of meat, then flip the piece of meat over by lifting it with the blade. Repeat until the meat is of the desired texture.
- To scrape: hold the cleaver firmly in one hand then run the sharp blade across a piece of meat/vegetable. This is useful for removing excess fat off a piece of meat.

Noodle Strainer

- Perfect for lifting noodles or draining food from a wok.

Entertaining Nonya Style

There is a strict code of practice when it comes to the selection of dishes and the presentation of a Nonya meal. The combination of dishes should have a perfect balance of contrasts. As a guideline, a typical Nonya menu should consist of a combination of the following:

- *Kuah putih* (white gravy dish) such as Chap Chai, Asam Putih, Kuah Ladah, Tauhu Titek and Ayam Goreng.
- *Kuah pedas* (red hot gravy dish) such as Ikan Pedas, Gulai Ikan, Ayam Kleo and Ayam Pedas.
- *Lauk piring* (individual dishes). This includes individual dishes from multiple-dish meals, such as Sayur Kangkung, Udang Asam Goreng, Sayur Lodeh or Opor Ayam.
- Soup such as Pong Tauhu, Hee Peow and Bawan Kepiting.
- Rice
- *Sambal belacan* (chilli)
- *Achar* (pickled vegetables) such as Penang Achar and Achar with Rempah.

For a simple meal, prepare a smaller number of *lauk piring*. Multiple-dish meals such as Nasi Lemak and Lontong, or one-dish meals such as Popiah are alternative Nonya menus.

Many Nonyas, like my late grandmother and my aunts, enjoy cooking for the entire extended family and would often invite friends over to join them. The traditional Peranakan way of presenting food is the *tok panjang* style which literally means 'long table'. In the olden days, the food would be laid out on a long table and the guests would take their turn at the table. It was considered rude to reach out for food so the daughters and daughters-in-law of the host would stand behind the guests to serve them. After a group of guests has finished eating, the table would be cleared and reset, in preparation for the next group of guests.

The table would be replenished from what seemed like an endless supply of food from the kitchen. It was considered an embarrassment to serve just enough food, so a good host always ensured that there was more than enough for everyone. This is still practised in some homes during Chinese New Year and Sunday family lunches, although less so during weddings and birthdays.

Peranakan Tableware

Peranakan tableware is very similar to Chinese porcelain tableware in terms of the shape and size of the spoons, bowls and plates. Tableware in pastel shades of yellow, pink, blue, green and turquoise with delicate and elaborate floral patterns are typically used.

Older generation Peranakans are very *pantang* (superstitious) and would avoid using blue and white-coloured serving plates, as these are their colours of mourning. Modern Peranakans, however, are generally less superstitious.

Peranakans traditionally ate using the fingers on their right hand, as with the Malay custom. The art to eating this way is to press the food lightly together using the tips of your fingers without letting it touch your palm. You then use your thumb to push the food into your mouth. Peranakans now eat their food with a fork and spoon.

Kum chings are porcelain jars with covers. The larger, more colourful ones are used to serve rice and soup, and the smaller ones are used to serve *achar*. Less elaborate blue and white jars are used in the kitchen to hold water.

Weights and Measures

Quantities for this book are given in Metric and American (spoon and cup) measures. Standard spoon and cup measurements used are: 1 teaspoon = 5 ml, 1 tablespoon = 15 ml, 1 cup = 250 ml. All measures are level unless otherwise stated.

LIQUID AND VOLUME MEASURES

Metric	Imperial	American
5 ml	$^1/_6$ fl oz	1 teaspoon
10 ml	$^1/_3$ fl oz	1 dessertspoon
15 ml	$^1/_2$ fl oz	1 tablespoon
60 ml	2 fl oz	$^1/_4$ cup (4 tablespoons)
85 ml	$2^1/_2$ fl oz	$^1/_3$ cup
90 ml	3 fl oz	$^3/_8$ cup (6 tablespoons)
125 ml	4 fl oz	$^1/_2$ cup
180 ml	6 fl oz	$^3/_4$ cup
250 ml	8 fl oz	1 cup
300 ml	10 fl oz ($^1/_2$ pint)	$1^1/_4$ cups
375 ml	12 fl oz	$1^1/_2$ cups
435 ml	14 fl oz	$1^3/_4$ cups
500 ml	16 fl oz	2 cups
625 ml	20 fl oz (1 pint)	$2^1/_2$ cups
750 ml	24 fl oz ($1^1/_5$ pints)	3 cups
1 litre	32 fl oz ($1^3/_5$ pints)	4 cups
1.25 litres	40 fl oz (2 pints)	5 cups
1.5 litres	48 fl oz ($2^2/_5$ pints)	6 cups
2.5 litres	80 fl oz (4 pints)	10 cups

DRY MEASURES

Metric	Imperial
30 grams	1 ounce
45 grams	$1^1/_2$ ounces
55 grams	2 ounces
70 grams	$2^1/_2$ ounces
85 grams	3 ounces
100 grams	$3^1/_2$ ounces
110 grams	4 ounces
125 grams	$4^1/_2$ ounces
140 grams	5 ounces
280 grams	10 ounces
450 grams	16 ounces (1 pound)
500 grams	1 pound, $1^1/_2$ ounces
700 grams	$1^1/_2$ pounds
800 grams	$1^3/_4$ pounds
1 kilogram	2 pounds, 3 ounces
1.5 kilograms	3 pounds, $4^1/_2$ ounces
2 kilograms	4 pounds, 6 ounces

OVEN TEMPERATURE

	°C	°F	Gas Regulo
Very slow	120	250	1
Slow	150	300	2
Moderately slow	160	325	3
Moderate	180	350	4
Moderately hot	190/200	370/400	5/6
Hot	210/220	410/440	6/7
Very hot	230	450	8
Super hot	250/290	475/550	9/10

LENGTH

Metric	Imperial
0.5 cm	$^1/_4$ inch
1 cm	$^1/_2$ inch
1.5 cm	$^3/_4$ inch
2.5 cm	1 inch

OTHER MEASURES

1 thumb size knob = 5 cm

ABBREVIATION

tsp	teaspoon
tbsp	tablespoon
g	gram
kg	kilogram
ml	millilitre
l	litre
min	minute(s)
hr	hour(s)